Nazeing History Work

Nazein

The Story of a House and its People

by

John H. Gervis

with additional material by
Margaret Gervis
and
John Walker

Published by
Nazeing Books

NB

Published for Dr John Gervis by Nazeing Books

Copies of this publication may be purchased, price £10 from
The Book Centre
24-26 Fawkon Walk
Hoddesdon
Hertfordshire
EN11 8TJ

ISBN 0-9511869-3- 0
Comments and enquiries concerning editorial content should be addressed to the author, whose home is the subject of this book.
Cover picture reproduced by kind permission of the artist, Alan Hart

Nazeing History Workshop, Publication No. 2

Nazeing History Workshop, Publication No. 1

David John Pracy
Not a Better Set in the Country:
Story of Nazeing Wood or Park, 1778-1950
published by Nazeing Conservation Society
August 1995, price £5
ISBN 0-9526048-1-7

Production by Peter Lardi
Printed in England

Contents

Introduction ~ Bibliography and Bouquets 5

1 Locale 10
2 The Structure of the House, by John Walker 17
3 Medieval Origins; Harold. The Abbot 23
4 The Manor Courts 31
5 King Henry VIII and Katherine Parr 37
6 The Dennys:
Anthony, Henry, Edward, Sir Ralph Sadler 41
7 Back to the House; Structure and Inhabitants 53
8 The Pilgrim Fathers; John Eliot 57
9 The Earls of Carlisle; James Hay, senior and junior 67
10 The Gorings; George, senior and junior, Charles 77
11 Nazeing Wood, Green Mead 83
12 The Jones Wake Takeover: 91
13 Nazeing Bury ~ 1600-1960 - Collins & Pegrum 101
14 1960 - The Gervis Arrival 117
15 General Practice 119
16 The Spirit of the House by Margaret Gervis 123
17 Conclusion 138

List of Illustrations and Maps 139

List of Appendix Material
i Chronological Tree 140
ii Nazeing Bury Owners and Tenants 144
iii The Vicarage and the Advowson 146

John and Margaret at the wedding of their youngest son, 1995

Introduction

Following our marriage in 1954, Margaret and I moved into our first home, a houseboat on the Thames. I was a medical student at St. Thomas' Hospital and had met my wife-to-be in the midwifery department, where she was furthering her own nursing training. Realising we would need somewhere to live, a boat seemed a good solution. It had been built as a troop landing craft for the Normandy invasion, forty feet long, square ended and flat bottomed it seemed ideal for conversion, having a roof although bereft of engines or any interior fittings. Moored at Cheyne Walk in the rather attractive yacht basin, it was conveniently situated for a daily cycle ride to the hospital.

So, prior to marriage, the next few months were rather busy studying for exams and in spare time converting this hull into a habitation. The result, achieved virtually on time, thanks to the valiant labours of friends and relations, was a most comfortable, but small, four roomed floating home.

The arrival of two daughters over the next two years necessitated building a nursery extension on the roof. With most congenial neighbours and a view of the Thames this boat, we called The Patriarch, served as an idyllic start to married life until career needs forced us to sell up and live a peripatetic existence for a couple of years.

In 1959 I joined the medical partnership of Drs. Freddie Beilby and Leslie Roe. Realising an outpost to the Hoddesdon practice, sited in Nazeing, should be set up, a Nazeing domicile was a condition imposed on the incoming partner.

We moved into rented accommodation and started to look for somewhere more permanent to settle, hopefully for life. We gradually became intrigued by a rather shabby looking, large house ideally situated for our and the practice needs. Discussing the matter with Ann Cayford she informed me the house belonged to her brothers who by good chance were trying to sell. Ann was what would nowadays be termed the practice manager, a truly splendid person, who pretty well managed everything in the practice.

Now with three children, we needed somewhere larger than a boat or our present semi, so we took the plunge and bought it. The house was **Nazeing Bury**. It was set well back from the main road in nearly an acre of wild garden bordered by a red brick wall with a large and venerable scots pine standing sentinel near the house. Faded stucco adorned by quoining and topped by a parapet with a central triangular pediment contributed to an effect of former grandeur. Six ground floor rooms and six and more bedrooms above were desperately in need of tender loving care.

We realised the house was old, quite how old no one seemed to know. Local lore had it that Catherine Parr had once lived there and been courted therein by King Henry VIII. Margaret who was rather intrigued by this legend spent several hours researching her history at the London Museum. We visited Sudely Castle where Catharine Parr had died and where many papers concerning her are kept, all to no avail. Further research had to wait, apart from the odd snippets of information, due to work and family pressures.

Following my retirement, in 1993, Margaret and I joined the **Nazeing History Workshop** which had been revitalised by Doug Ball. This has been a useful venue for the exchange of information and ideas. I intended actively to pursue research on the house but was diverted while keying into a computer database the Nazeing All Saints Parish records, which are contained in vellum bound volumes dating back to 1559. They provide a rather precious and fairly complete record of the births, deaths and marriages within the parish. I hoped to come across references to Nazeing Bury and did indeed find some, thus:

1576 "W. Southernewood. Mar 27 a poore boy found dead at Y Burry." - A glimpse of a tragedy.

Another bonus of exploring these books was acquiring a familiarity with old handwriting, a much needed asset when it came to tackling other documents.

Spelling in times past had not acquired its present fixed form. In the parish records for example "Nazeing" goes through various vicissitudes. Nazing in 1631, Nazeing in 1651 and Nasing for the next two hundred years. The spelling of surnames is also variable. These same comments apply to the rest of the primary source material. In this treatise I have more or less 'modernised' the spelling for the sake of readability.

Sources of Information. We had been aware for many years of a cache of papers kept at the Northampton Record Office relating to Nazeing Bury and these have formed the bulk of the material for this history. They consist of documents assembled by Isaac Jones and his son Sir Samuel during the 17th century in their multifarious dealings with the legacies of the Denny estates. The Jones and Wake families between them continued to add to these papers well into the twentieth century. Hence a splendid depository of information exists which is now conserved under the title of Wake, Courteenhall, where they can be viewed by request.

The above mentioned were all in their turn Lords of the Manor of Nazeing. Now an honorary title, it once denoted land ownership which brought legal disputations and dispositions in its train.

Joan Wake daughter of Sir Herewald, the twelfth baronet, devoted much of her life to ensuring the preservation of historical documents of relevance to Northamptonshire. Apart from the safety of her own family documents she scoured the county amassing over the years much other material of general relevance. This she finally managed to have stored and catalogued in Delapre Abbey. Several years later it was all rehoused in the new purpose built Northampton Record Office.

Bibliography

Some of these Wake documents are written on parchment bearing elaborate headings and waxen seals, scribed in a generally fairly legible hand, in Latin, English or both. Many pieces are copies of earlier documents, made at the behest of Jones and various of the Wakes. These are mostly countersigned as being authentic, as is for example that of Richard I's edict given at Nonancourt.

A further most useful and very readable source has been Professor Peter Gordon's book: *The Wakes of Northamptonshire*. This gives a graphic account of the few Jones and many Wakes and their background and family seat at Courteenhall. It also unravels how the Wakes came to be the Lords of The Manor of Waltham and Nazeing.

Antonia Fraser's admirable book: *Cromwell Our Chief of Men*, gives a vivid account of the Civil War and also features several of the personalities who appear in this parochial tale of Nazeing.

Katherine Parr and her era are vividly brought to life by Anthony Martienssen in his book: *Queen Katherine Parr.*

The *Victoria County History* is an amazing mine of information of which I have made considerable use.

Morant's *History and Antiquities of the County of Essex* written in 1768 has some interesting information, as also does Collar's *History of Essex*, published in 1866. For example he writes the following concerning Nazeing church: "A small door behind one of the columns opens on a winding stair leading to a niche in front of the chancel. Here it is believed offenders were made to do penance by public exposure expiating their crimes." The present incumbent, Martin Webster, claims ignorance of this custom.

The Dictionary of National Biography, has been another indispensable reference work.

County Record Offices have been helpful. An early find at Chelmsford was the document recording that Katherine's mother, Maud Parr, had leased a tract of land in Nazeing from the Abbots of Waltham - an exciting find which spurred us on and did at last explain some connection of the Parrs with Nazeing.

John Walker has devoted many hours to measuring and recording the structure of Nazeing Bury, as witness his monograph in chapter 2, which has added a further welcome dimension to this book and contributed to my understanding of the house, even if we have differed at times! Thank you John.

I am especially grateful to David Pracy, a founder member of the Nazeing History Workshop and a post-graduate student of the University of Essex, for his invaluable help in the gestation of this work. Apart from assisting in the conversion of my doctor's staccato English into something resembling literary English, which has involved reading through several drafts, he has also helped locate much useful source material and produced stimulating ideas on the past history of Nazeing.

David and Merylyn Shaw, as also David Mort, have kindly read and corrected proofs.

Chapter 1

Locale

Nazeing is a rather spread out village of some five thousand inhabitants, sited on the western border of Essex. The river Lea marks its boundary with Hertfordshire. West of and parallel to the river runs the railway adjacent to the towns of Broxbourne and Hoddesdon. Some five miles to the South is Waltham Abbey whilst Roydon lies to the North and the new town of Harlow to the East.

The 'upper town' of Nazeing is situated on a promontory of higher ground north east of the Nazeing Brook. 'Nase' is the Saxon word for nose, a projection, which probably explains the origin of the name, although there is some dispute on this point. Here are generally older houses and also the parish church of All Saints.

This church has gradually increased in size since its foundation in the 12th century. It is an attractive building of red brick and flint. The tower was also added in stages but its spire had to be removed in 1899. There are currently [1997] plans afoot to provide a general purpose room, to be known as The Pilgrim Room, together with other facilities.

The house presently known as **Nazeing Bury** stands in 'Lower Nazeing,' adjoining the old water meadows. This flat area, on the eastern bank of the River Lea, had been liable to recurrent flooding from late medieval times, hence there were few early habitations hereabouts. Nowadays, following the construction of a flood relief channel, much of this land, the original 'meadows, woods and wastes,' is occupied by houses, shops and commercial greenhouses. The rest has been exploited for its rich gravel reserves, followed by infilling and the creation of lakes. This parkscaping, under the beneficial influence of the Lee Valley Regional Park Authority has, to a considerable extent, ameliorated the previous depradations.

The house itself, formerly adjoined by several farm buildings and an orchard, lies N.W. of the Nazeing crossroads, an intersection known to have existed from at least 1404 and then marked by 'Le Bery Cross,' with which is associated a certain William le Bery or William at Bury - a rather sketchy figure known to have lived around this date and to have possessed several houses in the area, including the Bury at Nazeing, hence perhaps his own name.

This leads us to linguistics. From where does the suffix Bery or Bury derive? The Oxford Dictionary unequivocally defines Bury as meaning a 'manor house or large farm.' Morant goes further suggesting it signifies 'a town, or capital seat where the Lord's court was kept.' Several towns and villages here and elsewhere have manor houses named in this fashion, such as Harlowbury and Claverhambury in both of which courts were formerly held.

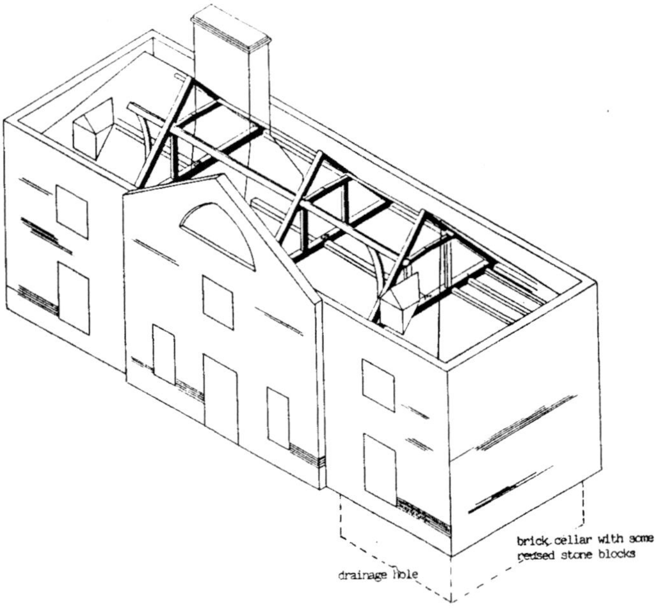

Fig 1: Nazeingbury late 17th century after walls rebuilt in brick

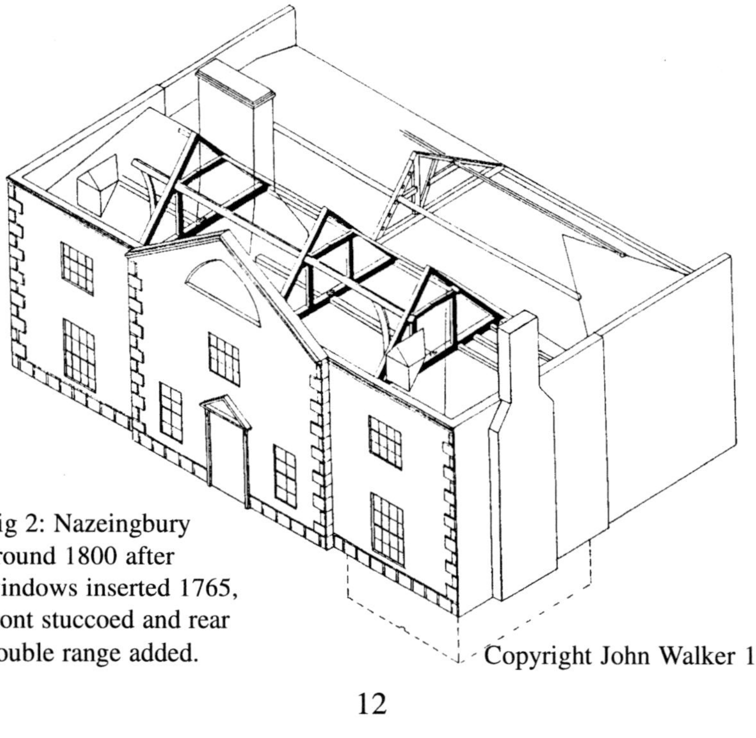

Fig 2: Nazeingbury around 1800 after windows inserted 1765, front stuccoed and rear double range added.

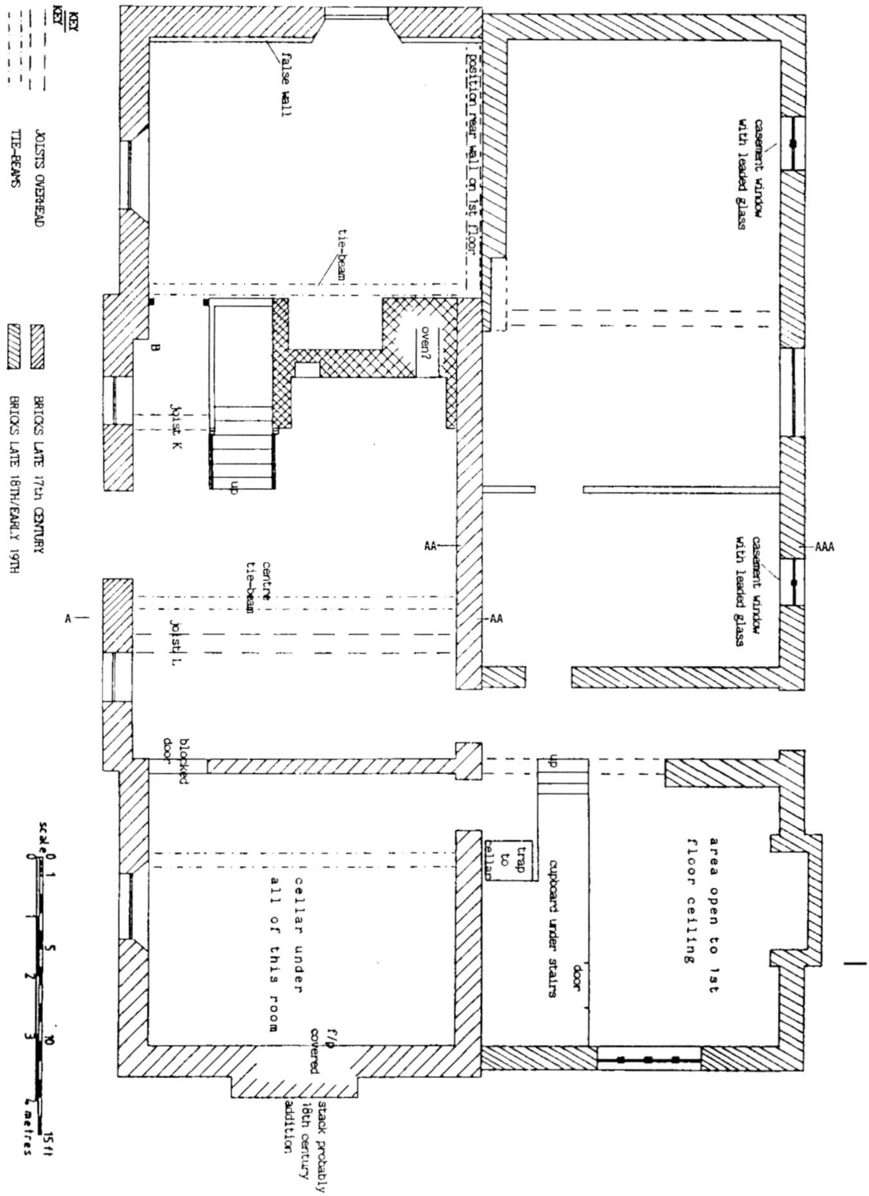

Fig 3: Ground Plan of Nazeingbury January 1997

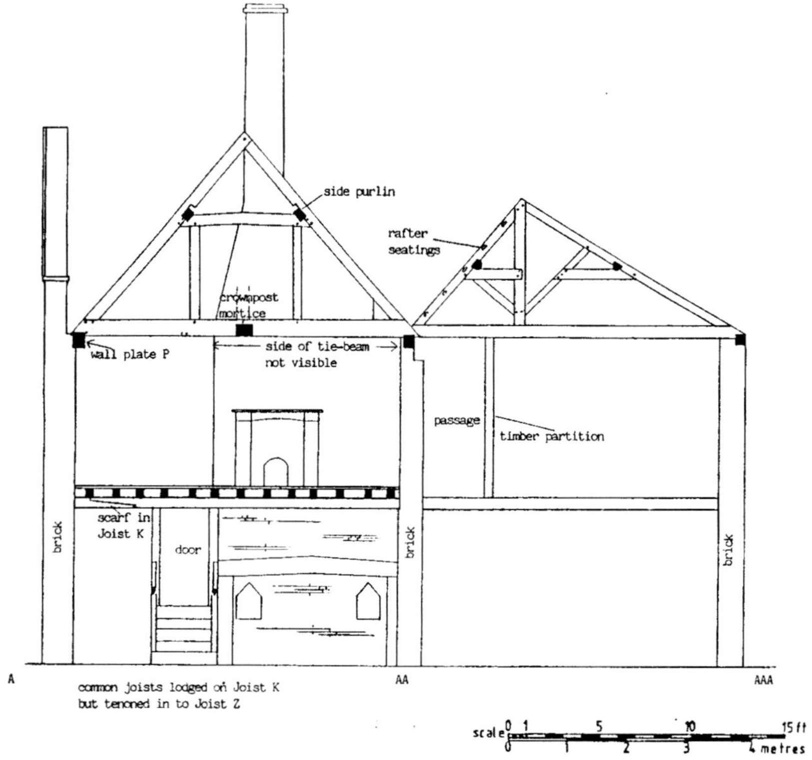

Fig 4: Cross section of Nazeingbury

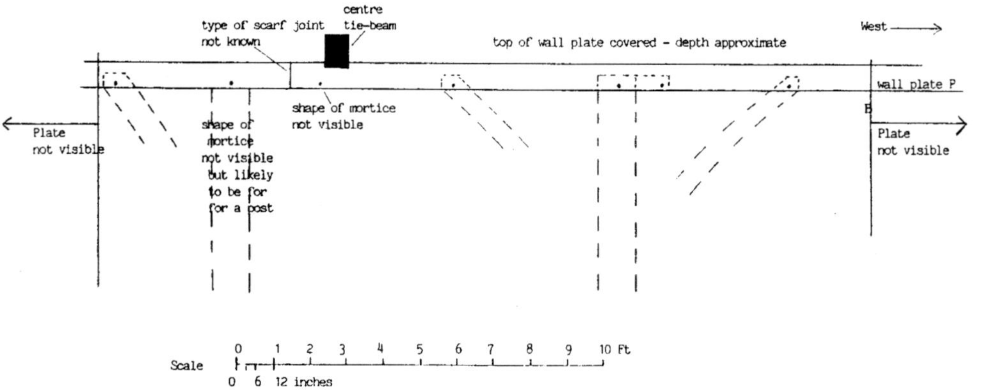

Fig 5: Wall plate P across south projecting bay showing empty mortices
Plate is reused from an aisled building

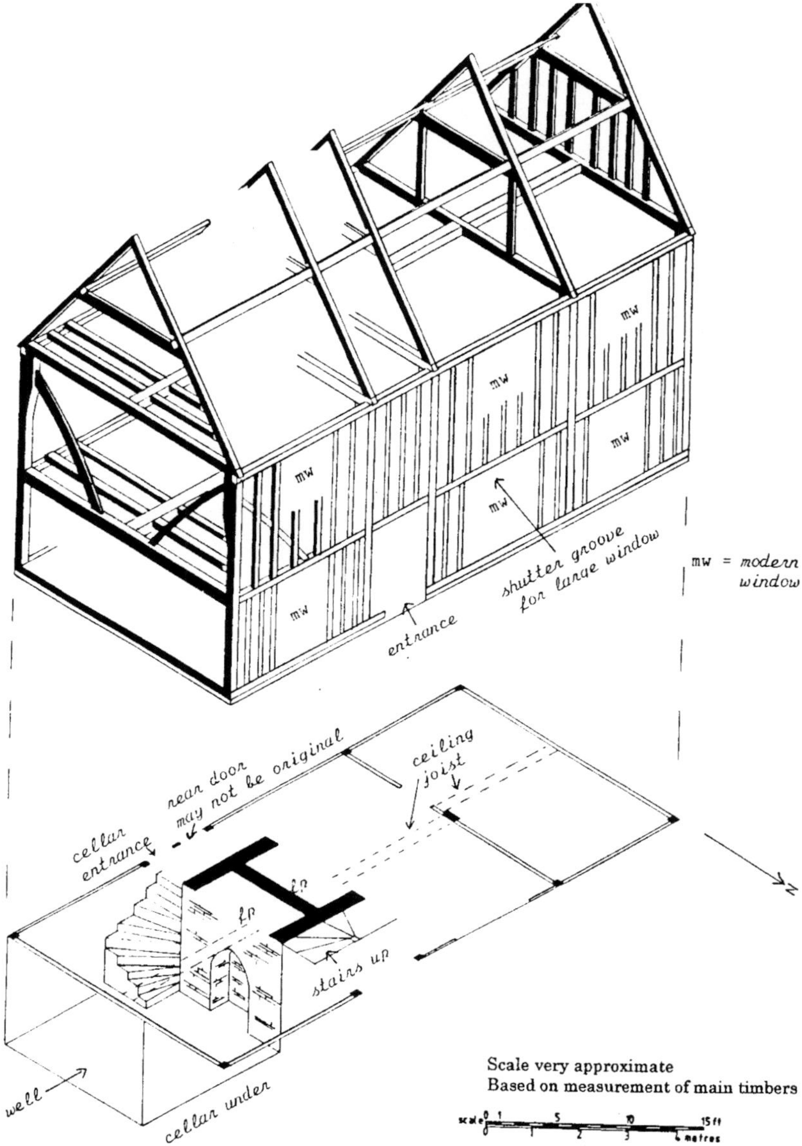

Fig 6: Cutlands, St Leonards Road Nazeing, Essex Map ref TL 389058

Late 16th or early 17th century lobby entrance house, two storey and attic with stairs in front of chimney stack. Studs on ground floor are closer together than on first floor suggesting exterior was originally covered in plaster. Has internal tension bracing halved across the inside of the studs. Ground floor rooms either side of stack and first floor room to left were heated.

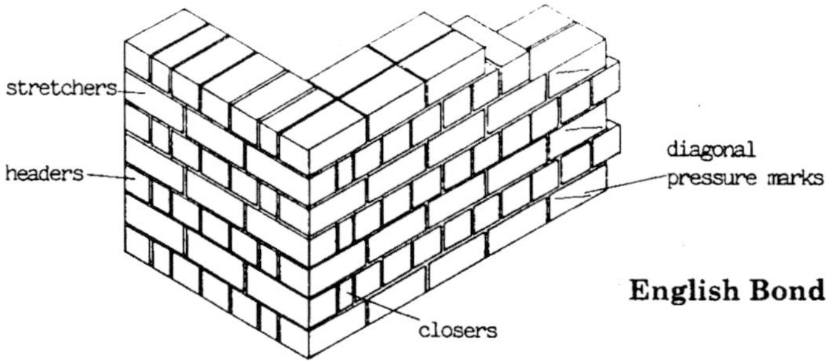

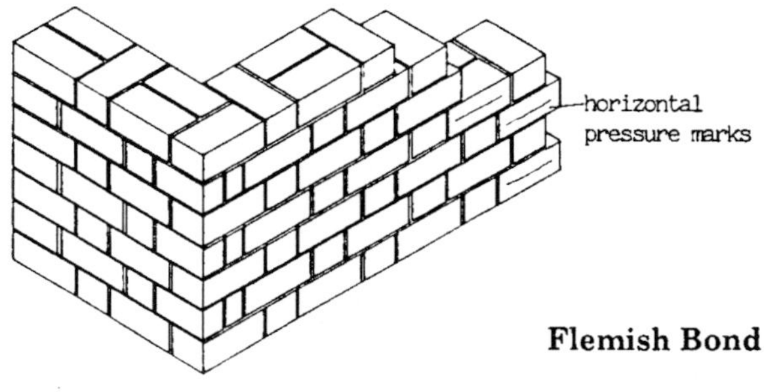

Fig 7: English and Flemish Brick Bonds

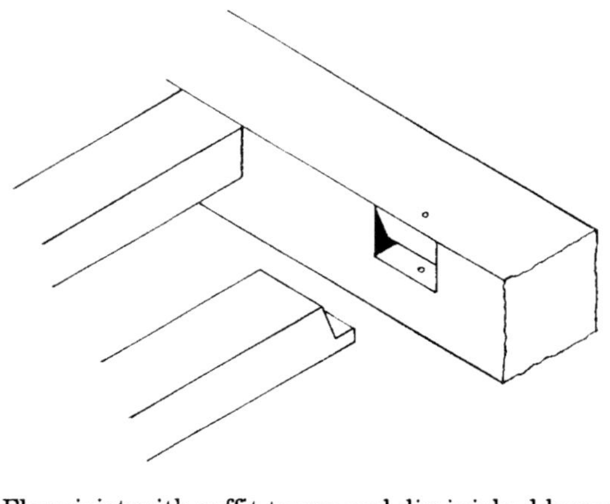

Fig 8: Floor joist with soffit tenon and diminished haunch

This joint appears in 1510-12 & rapidly becomes the standard in the 16th C

Chapter 2 Structure of The House

by John Walker

Nazeing Bury is a two storey timber framed house, encased in brick in the 1670-80s and given a pedimented projecting front bay (fig. 1). Internally it appears to have retained the 16th century plan. In 1765 it was updated with vertical sliding sash windows, the front and sides covered in stucco and plaster quoins added down the corners of the building (fig. 2). During the latter half of the 18th century, or very early 19th a second brick range was added along the rear, making the house double piled (fig. 2). Of the timber framed house little is visible, but documentary evidence suggests that some time before 1569 both the ground and first floors were heated by a chimney, probably the present chimney.

Medieval and 16th Century Building

Very little is known of the medieval house that occupied the site. The lease granted to John Nankotton in 1502 by the Abbot of Waltham states that the Manor Court is to be held in the house and that Nankotton shall: 'repair and maintain all the buildings and walls with covering of the same, thatch, plaster'. (see chapter 3)

This may indicate that the original roof covering of the house was thatch. Based on other surviving manor houses it would have had a central hall, open to the roof and heated by an open hearth. This would have been entered from outside by opposing doorways at one end of the hall, probably the east end (see below), forming what is called a cross passage. This is called the low end of the hall, and below the passage on the east side would have been two small service rooms for the storage of food and drink, with a single first floor chamber above. There would have been an external kitchen, to which there is reference in the inventory of 1502.

John Ramsey's will of 1568 tells us that the west ground floor room was called the Parlour and that there was a heated chamber above. He stipulated that his:

> 'wife should have 1 year's abiding in a chamber over the parlour on the west end of the house which I dwell in, with free ingress and regress, and with meat, bread and drink of the best and firewood ready prepared to her hand freely'. 1
> (see chapter 7)

This suggests the first floor chamber was heated by a chimney, and by implication that the parlour below was also heated. If this was by the chimney which survives today, then the hall was also heated. There also may have been a floor above the hall as the joint used in the present floor joist, a soffit tenon with diminished haunch, first appears early in the 16th century and becomes almost the standard joint by the second quarter of the same century (see fig. 8)2

This building could have been the old medieval house updated by the insertion of the chimney stack and a floor into the open hall, or a completely new house. Its plan would either have retained the cross-passage at the low end of the hall, or would have moved it to opposite the chimney stack, creating a layout very similar to Cutlands, St. Leonards Road, Nazeing (fig.6). This form becomes popular from the 1570's onwards.

Late 17th Century Improvements

In the late 17th century, say in 1670s/1680s, the house was encased in brick, given a projecting pedimented middle bay, the front door moved to the middle giving a fashionable symmetrical front (fig. 1). It was probably re-roofed at this time.

The suggested date is based on the type of bricks and the use of English bond, plus the style of the front, which was being used for larger houses from at least the 1670's. Inigo Jones produced designs of a symmetrical house with a pedimented front for the Prince's Lodgings in 1619-22. [3] (Chambers, 79). It is used for Tring Manor House, Hertfordshire and Winslow Hall, Buckingham in 1669 (Chambers, 98); Hatley Park, Cambridgeshire ca 1700. [4] (Burke's 18); in Essex at Dynes Hall, Gt. Maplestead 1690's (Burke's 48), Dytchleys, South Weald 1729 (Burke's 49), Lyston Hall, Liston ca 1730 (Burke's 62), Walton's, Barlow End ca 1730 (Burke's 78).

Soft $2^{1}/_{4}$ inch wide bricks are used, laid in English bond with rubbed bricks forming a flat vousoir over the windows. English bond (fig. 7) was used in the 16th century, and from the 1630's was slowly replaced through the 17th century by Flemish bond (fig. 7) with the latter becoming the main bond in the 18th century. However English bond came back into use in the second half of the 18th century, if indeed it ever entirely ceased to be used, and was used in a small way by the Victorians. There were no quoins down the corners of the building at this stage - these were added in plaster in the 18th century.

Behind the new front, the plan of the building remained unchanged, except that one now entered directly into the middle of the hall. This arrangement was not uncommon, particularly when older buildings were altered. Greenleaves in Nazeing, partly a medieval house, moved its main entrance in the 17th or 18th century to the centre of the front, presumably to give a symmetrical front, giving direct entry into the hall. A similar plan evolved at Battles Hall, Manuden when the ground floor was rebuilt in brick in the late 17th / early 18th century. The cellar under the east room may have been added at this time as it is brick lined. However it could be late 16th century as it has some reused stone blocks in the walls; these may have come from the Abbey and been supplied by Lord Edward Denny when he was building his house in Waltham Abbey around 1590.

It is not known how much of Nazeing Bury's original timber frame survives within the brickwork. It was probably reroofed with its present clasped side purlin roof (fig. 4) at the same time as the walls were rebuilt in brick. The rafters are reused from a collar rafter roof, and some are smoke blackened suggesting they are from a medieval open hall. The three tie-beams are reused. The dovetail at the south end of the central tie-beam has been recut about 2 inches from the original end of the beam, cutting into the former mortice for the jowl of the principal post below the tie-beam. The other tie-beams cannot be examined in detail but appear to be identical to the central beam. All three have a central mortice for a crown post, none appear to be smoke blackened and all three had no partition above them. They probably come from a high quality barn; if they were from the original house, only one, or at most two, would have been open, the other forming part of the closed partition at the end of the hall. In addition the central tie-beam bears no relation to the empty mortices in the south wall plate which is visible only across the projecting pedimented bay (fig.5). This plate comes from an aisled building, and probably timbers from an aisled barn have been used for part of the roof.

The updating of the house is more pretentious than necessary for a yeoman farmer; it is for someone aspiring to Gentleman status, and raises the question of who built it, the tenant or the owner. It is unlikely to be the owner unless the house was visible from his house or he could use it to attract a tenant prepared to pay a higher rent. The plan behind the facade remains that of a yeoman farmhouse, and thus less attractive to a Gentleman, making it more likely to be built by the tenant as part of the conditions of his lease. On the other hand, where information is available on leases for Nazeing Bury in the 18th century, they are granted for only 15 years, and if the same applied in the 17th century this would have made it less attractive economically for the tenant to have overspent on the upgrading.

Improvements Second Half of 18th Century

The front was upgraded with new windows in 1765 when an invoice lists 20 days' work, timber, battening deale, nails etc.and including **sash timber.** The existing sash windows, with their 8 lights, each $16^1/_2$ by $10^1/_2$ inches wide and thin $^5/_8$ inch glazing bars, fit well with this date. They were exactly the same size as the early windows as indicated by small closure half bricks, visible down the sides of the windows when part of the stucco was repaired in 1986 (See photo p 100). Probably at the same time the front was covered in stucco and imitation plaster quoins added down the corners of the front. (fig.2). A rear brick range was added along the back, doubling the size of the house, probably in the early 1800's since an 1807 George III penny was found under one of the window frames. The brick is laid, as on the front, in English bond. It could be slightly earlier as the bricks have diagonal pressure marks which are more common on 17th and 18th century bricks than 19th. The latter tend to have horizontal marks (fig. 7) [5] (Ryan 92). Also the bricks are $8^1/_2$ by $2^1/_2$ inches, the size more common around the middle of the 18th century. Bricks are around 8 by $2^1/_4$ inches in the 17th and early 18th century, getting larger through the century, being $8^1/_2$ by $2^1/_2$ inches around the middle of the century and nearer $8^3/_4$ by $2^1/_2$ by the close.

It is difficult now to determine the purpose of this expansion. (but see chapter 13). The north-east room may well have been a rear kitchen/wash house, bringing into the house functions which had been carried out in a detached building. The rest of the ground floor was unheated and was either one room or divided as now into two by a timber partition (fig. 3). Windows appear to have been casements with leaded lights; there are two upper rear sash windows, smaller and in a different style to the front windows.

1 Emmison F G 1983, *Elizabethan Wills of South-West Essex* Kylin Press

2 Hewett C A 1980, *English Historic Carpentry*, Phillimore

3 Chambers J 1985, *The English House*, Thames Methuen

4 Montgomery-Massingberd H ed 1981, *Burke's & Savills Guide to Country Houses Vol III East Anglia* (Cited as Burke's in text).

5 Ryan, Pat 1996, *Bricks in Essex*

Chapter 3 Medieval Origins

Sometime between the 7th and 9th centuries there existed a nunnery on the meads between Nazeing Bury and the river Lea. It was an outpost of the Abbey at Barking and was for tending the sick, having been been founded at the instigation of Suebred who at that time was the king of Essex. He put this nunnery in charge of one of his female relations who was later probably buried within the curtilage of the little church. Recently Mr P Huggins who excavated this site has suggested that this was part of a local complex incorporating Nazeing and Roydon and bounded on the south by the minster lands of Waltham.[1] This would add confirmation to the suggestion that a farm was sited where Nazeing Bury now stands, under the jurisdiction of this nunnery, to supply it with labour and food.[2] It is possible this little community was overrun by the Vikings towards the end of the first millennium.

The more certain historical record commences with **Harold the Earl of Wessex** who believed himself to have been cured of a stroke by laying hands on the Holy Cross of Waltham. This cross, on account of its reputed healing ability, had been installed in a church built to receive it at Waltham by one Tovi, a wealthy landowner in about 1030. Following this healing the church and the surrounding lands were granted to Harold by Edward the Confessor, his brother in law, whereupon he founded there a new and larger church. This was dedicated in the presence of King Edward in 1060.

Harold also endowed a college at Waltham comprising a dean in charge of twelve secular canons, for the maintenance of which he designated Northland, an estate of 360 acres including the Manor of Waltham. Each canon was assigned 15 acres of this estate. In addition they were granted seventeen other rather widely scattered manors, all under the jurisdiction of the newly appointed Dean of Waltham, acting in his capacity as the Lord of the Manor; one of which was in Nazeing.

I get the impression that Harold chose established demesnes likely to assist the material needs of the college and its canons. The houses themselves would have been timber framed buildings infilled with wattle and daub.

All this Harold organized just four years before his death at the battle of Hastings in 1066. Following which his body is reputed to have been brought back and buried at Waltham, the site of this being now marked in the churchyard.[3]

After the conquest, all of Harold's land in Waltham, including most of the Northland estate, as well as his land to the north as far as Harolds Park in Nazeing - incidentally almost certainly named after him - passed to William the Conqueror who in turn in 1075 granted it to Walcher, Bishop of Durham, thus providing the bishop with a seat and staging post near London.[4]

The canons of Waltham held 600 acres in Nazeing, which included 13 acres of meadow and half a fishery. This included the manor of Nazeing granted to the canons by Harold which at the time of Domesday employed five 'villeins' and two borders. These would have inhabited their own tenements but been entirely subject to the demands of the lord as passed down via the freeman of the manor.

The Victoria County History equates this manor with Nazeingbury, later the presumed residence of William le Bery and the site perhaps of a still earlier dwelling serving the former nunnery.

The canons were probably not too much disturbed by William's arrival apart from some diminution of their property and the manorial system continued. In 1108 Maud, Queen to Henry I, granted them the return of their Northland estate in exchange for some land in Aldgate.

Harold's college continued in being but during a fracas in

1144 the canons' houses in Waltham were burned down.

In 1177 Henry II as an atonement for the murder of Thomas Becket vowed to build an abbey of regular canons which he did at Waltham, the sitting tenants being paid off and replaced by ordained canons, for whom a new abbey was opened by the king in 1184. He also provided for the rebuilding of the church which was finally rededicated in 1242.

After the death of his father Henry II, Richard I in 1189 at Nonancourt directed that:

> 'All our Manor of Waltham with the great Wood and with the Park, which is called Harold's Park, to be enclosed and had as a park to the Church of the Holy Cross of Waltham and the use of the canons. . . that they may most freely and quietly serve God . . . And with all woods and wastes and with three hundred acres of assarts in the same Manor and with the market . . . and the village of Nesinges which appertains to the aforesaid Manor . . . And with all wastes and woods and with . . . one hundred and sixty acres of assarts in the same vill . . .to hold of us . . . for ever . .rendering . .yearly for all service sixty pounds.'[4]

This gift was perhaps in part to appease his father's memory and also to please his mother, Eleanor of Aquitaine. He had not excelled in his filial duties.

This large domain comprising the great manor of Waltham was retained and administered by the Abbey until its dissolution in 1540. Some exchanges of land took place, much of which had been owned in surrounding areas. Churches and manors were also possessed in several other counties including Wormley Church in Hertfordshire and Copped Hall Manor. There were times of hardship, times of plague and times of friction and revolt between Abbey, townspeople and peasants.

Documentation is fragmentary for the next four hundred

years but a parchment written in 1502 relating to the Manor of Nazeing is preserved. This is the document already referred to by John Walker in chapter 2 and is an indenture written in Latin recording the lease by Alan, the Abbot of Waltham, of the Manor of Nasing to John Nankotton.[5] A free transcription of this lease reads as follows:

> This indenture witnesses that Alan, Abbot of the monastery of the Holy Cross of Waltham and the convent there has handed over to farm to John Nankotton of London, merchant, the manor of Nasyng in the county of Essex with all the arable, meadow and pasture lands and the rights of pasture. Also the tithes of the rectory together with its fruits and produce. To be reserved for the abbot and his successors shall be the fixed rents and appurtenances of the office of kitchener of the monastery as also the perquisites of the court, the woods and underwoods and the forfeits granted the abbot by the charter of the lord king.
>
> The said John, his executors and assigns, is to have the manor together with the tithes and fruits aforesaid but excepting the aforementioned. This to commence from the feast of St. Michael next for thirty one years paying in respect thereof thirty two pounds of legal money of England by equal portions at two terms of the year, Easter and St Michael. The said John shall bear the secular and ecclesiastical charges of the manor. He shall also repair and maintain all the buildings and walls with covering of the same, thatch, plaster. Will also clear away, make and repair the hedges, ditches and watering places for stock as often as is necessary at his own expense. To take nothing from the trees or hedges growing there beyond haybote, cartbote and ploughbote, which is to say thorns, firewood and wood for the repairing of carts and ploughs. All this for the inspection of the cellarer or other appointee of the abbot.

At the end of his term John or his executors will hand over all the buildings well and sufficiently repaired.

Each year he shall provide for the cellarer and steward, together with their servants and horses, necessary and decent food as often as is necessary for holding the court there or for supervising works due on the manor or for receiving rent from the farm.

He shall use manure collected from the farm on the demesne lands of the manor and not elsewhere.

Nor shall he or his executors at the end of his term remove from the manor doors, windows or anything else fixed there with mortar, lead or nails of wood or iron.

He shall appear before the auditor of the monastery once in the year on the day appointed for rendering his account under penalty for default of six shillings and eight pence.

At the end of his term John or his executors shall deliver back to the abbot the entire manor without diminution to the lands, which shall be manured fallowed and reploughed, together with the live and dead stock or the fixed value of same.

If it happens that the annual payment be in arrears by one month after any of the aforesaid feasts then it shall be lawful for the abbot to enter the manor there to distrain and take away those things distrained and the same John to be expelled from the manor.

John Nankotton, Francis Foster gentlemen and William Larke, citizen and draper of London are bound to the abbot in one hundred marks of legal money of England. Provided John and his executors hold to these provisions then this bond shall be had for naught.

In witness of which matter both the common seal of the abbot and the seal of John Nankotton, Francis Foster and William Larke have been interchangeably afffixed to these indentures.

Given in our house and chapter in the 17th year of the reign of King Henry VII on the 29 day of January.

An inventory of all the goods and chattels, both live and dead, of the lord Alan, abbot received on the 29 January 1502 by John Nankotton, now farmer of Nasyng by surrender and delivery of George Congreve farmer of Nasyng:

23 cows	value 8s 3d	Dead stock; 13 qrt of wheat
1 bull		10 qtr of oats
3 mares	20s	hay, straw, grain
1 sow	2s 6d	
6 piglets	12d	
2 peacocks	male and female	
1 cock and 3 hens		

In the kitchen: 1 lead cistern within the dairy. 1 great brassn dish

All this is really quite informative. It tells us that at the beginning of the 16th century and presumably for at least a few years before that, George Congreve as tenant had been farming the lands of the Manor of Nazeing.

The livestock together with the arable land would have provided the basis of a thriving little farmstead. George's accommodation would have consisted of the medieval hall with its offshoots; in which the courts had been held from the 13th century, of which more anon.

The fact that the cellarer or other factotum was a regular visitor suggests considerable integration with abbey affairs, much as it had probably been when Harold first set up his system five centuries earlier. Thus the produce went to the monks. A very organised sounding little ecosystem, even to the disposition of the manure.

Whether John Nankotton the London merchant retired to Nazeing Bury to farm or alternatively leased this holding to tenant farmers, as the Lords of the Manor continued to do down the ages, we know not; neither do we know if he saw out his tenancy which would have expired shortly before the Dissolution.

1 P.J.Huggins. *Excavation of Belgic and Romano British Farm at Nazeingbury*, 1975. and *Nazeingbury 20 Years On.*

2 Colin Dauris *Nazeing Parish News*. Sept. 1996

3 Although an article in *The Times* in 1996 suggested he may have been buried near Hastings.

4 *Victoria County History*, henceforward: VCH, Vol V p155

5 Northampton Record Office. Wake, Courteenhall, hereinafter known as Wake.Document 157

6 Wake 160

The last Court Leet held under the Court Maple near Nazeing Church, 1925

Chapter 4 The Manor Courts

The Manor Courts feature as an integral part of the manor of Nazeing Bury from the 13th to late in the 19th century. The Public Record Office, now at Kew, holds the earliest documents relating to the court at Nasing comprising six pages, the court roll for the year 1270, each of 12 by 36 inches, of well preserved thin parchment written in a medieval script. Each section is headed by the date and twelve names which Margaret and I found impressive to view but quite unintelligible. Fortunately the Rev. Sutherland's booklet[1] contains some extracts which give a flavour of the matters brought to the courts at that time as quoted below. A few records also exist for the 15th Century, again written in the same script. I am told that the court rolls for Wales for this period have a similar format, a measure of the organisation existing within the British Isles even then.

The 1502 indenture already mentioned refers to courts held at the manor which the new leaseholder John Nankotton was to facilitate, even though the fees went to the monks. Records of courts held during these times are missing but mention is made in a document of 1541, a year after Waltham Abbey was dissolved, to the profits of the courts and leets,[2] thus I think it safe to assume that the practice continued.

Copies of some of the court proceedings during the 1630's are extant and there exists fragmentary evidence of courts for the years 1641 to 1650. From 1669 a virtually continuous record is extant until the beginning of this century of the proceedings of the courts held at Nazeing Bury, as well as at Waltham Abbey and Roydon Hamlet.

These meticulous records are preserved either as rolls - the court rolls, or carefully inscribed into leather bound volumes - the fair copy undertaken by the clerk from his minutes. In this respect the Manors of Nazeing and Waltham Holy Cross are fortunate in having such a complete record. Most of these are now kept at the Northampton Record Office. The Essex Office has microfilm of courts or drafts of same from 1670-1767.

Generally legibility is good, but in Latin until around 1733.

Typically the accounts of these courts are headed in the following manner in flowery script:

'The Manor of Nazeing in the County of Essex. Court Baron of . . Lord of the said Manor being held in and for the said manor.' Occasionally the clerk has added ebullient decorative scroll work, perhaps needing a change from his rather monotonous task. Apart from writing up these minutes he would often have to repeat them severally to the concerned parties. I possess an indenture dated 1795, being a copy to the litigant of the court proceedings of that date, and very involved it is!

The courts, the so called courts baron or leet, were held in the name of the Lord of the Manor, in this case the abbot of Waltham Abbey before the Dissolution and the secular lord subsequently, his steward undertaking the presiding role. The 'leet' being a jury of some twelve named locals; there might also be in attendance the 'homage' consisting of two or three copyholding freemen of the village. The same names of these long suffering members recur from year to year, some of whom even combined these duties with that of church warden. The tradition of public service goes back a long way.

The function of the courts was both administrative and judicial. A regular duty was the appointing of two constables and two pindars for the village. Keeping tabs on property was necessary since it ultimately belonged to the Lord of the Manor who leased it to his many tenants through their copyholding rights, the copy comprising the documents of the court. It was thus necessary to report deaths as this might entail transfer of tenancies and wills since copyholders were entitled to specify to whom their holdings should be granted. The dereliction of tenements led to the tenants being threatened with fines or eviction if matters were not put right. New copyholders would be admitted to their tenancies on payment of a 'fine' - a fee.

Rules concerning land and stock management and grazing rights on the common featured large and the following preamble is written into the minutes of the courts throughout the 18th and 19th C.

> The house holders of Nazeing Great Bury and Nazeing Little Bury are not to common in any of the commons upon forfeit of forty shillings.
>
> [Similar restrictions were placed on Nazeing Lodge and the Vicaridge.]
>
> No person shall put above 4 great cattle or 20 sheep upon forfeit of 10 shillings.
>
> No mangy horse or diseased beast upon forfeit of 10 shillings
>
> No stoned horse or colt larger than 14 hands upon forfeit of 10 shillings
>
> It is the custom to have a bull a boar and a stallion kept at Nazeing Great Bury for the use of the tenants of Nazeing at the charge of the Lord of the Manor.

The subject of tithes also features in these documents, it being important to make clear the custom due the vicarage such as one tenth of the yield of corn - a tythe, and in 1698 and in the years following 3 pence for example for a milch cow.

The other, judicial function of these courts necessitated the attendance of the leet and minor misdemeanors were judged, major felonies being tried increasingly at higher courts. In 1270 a man was fined for abusive words, a woman for selling ale and a farmer for putting up a stile.This last tended to be a recurring problem. Defamation was also deemed worthy of a fine, as it still is! And much other behaviour resulted in a forfeit such as letting the water out of the church pond, not sweeping a bridge or indeed for building a bridge.

The courts also adjudicated in cases of legal doubt, ownership of property often causing contention, the repetitiousness of the written records tending to further confuse matters. I am told the clerks were paid per word written which maybe accounts for this.

Although tedious to peruse, these documents contain an invaluable history of village affairs. Many properties are mentioned by name as are the names of the copyholding tenants and their adjacent fields. I found surprising the number of copyholders living elsewhere, generally in London, who sublet their properties.

I suspect the survival of Nazeing Bury as a dwelling place owes not a little to its function as the locale for these courts, which were a necessary part of community life. As a bonus they provided some income to its owner thus motivating him to keep it in repair. I find it a salutary thought that from the very early days of the open hall to the more recent era of an enclosed room on the very same site, these proceedings took place in the hall we know so well.

By the end of the last century, by which time Nazeing Bury no longer belonged to the Lord of the Manor, courts relating to the Manor of Nazeing were sometimes held at Lincolns Inn and by the beginning of this century held increasingly at the offices of Jessopp and Gough and other solicitors in Waltham Abbey.

The rather delightful photograph taken in 1925 depicts Mr Jessopp under the 'court maple' near Nazeing church surrounded by local worthies on the occasion of the last court. I am told by Peter Brent, who is well versed in village affairs, that it was the custom then for this court to meet once a year under this tree.

As a postscript to this chapter on the courts it happens that my son Nigel also lives in a house, near Brecon, where once the courts were held, as he and his wife Joyce have recently discovered.

1 Rev.Sutherland. *The History of Nazeing*

2 Wake 163, 167 - 'The leets of the manor to Anthony Denny. Rent £31 - 18.'

Maud Parr Indenture - 1527

Reproduced by kind permission of Essex Record Office

Chapter 5

King Henry VIII and Katherine Parr

This chapter, rather irrelevant to the story of Nazeing Bury, is prompted by the Nazeing folkstory, quoted in several local guides, that Henry courted Katherine, his last queen, whilst she resided at Nasingberry. Sadly we have been unable to substantiate this. Nevertheless there is good evidence that the king was familiar with the locality.

At Waltham he had stabling together with a forge for the use of his horses and carriages, this being a convenient servicing point on the journey from London to the North. The site of this forge can still be viewed in the Abbey Gardens.

Just North of Waltham Abbey he had been given Dallance, a house surrounded by Waltham Park which the King had landscaped towards the end of his reign, Sir Anthony Denny, amongst his other tasks, acting as its keeper.

He is known to have hunted in Epping Forest which extended into Nazeing Common, where he had another of his several hunting lodges, sited at Green Mead on the north eastern boundary.

Sir Thomas Parr, Katherine's father, was the controller of King Henry's household and one of his trusted servants. He was descended from Ivo de Tollebois, the first baron of Kendal and in 1508 he married Matilda Green, known as Maud, when she was but thirteen years of age. She was the daughter and co-heiress of Sir Thomas Green of Borton and Green's Norton in the county of Northamptonshire a descendant of the Talbots and Throckmortons.[1]

The Parrs lived largely in London, having a house at Blackfriars. They had three children, all of whom were probably born at Blackfriars, being conveniently near their place of palatial duties at Whitehall. Katherine the eldest was born around 1514, Ann in about 1515 and finally William a year later.

Sir Thomas died in 1517 and was buried at Blackfriars. His wife, aged only twenty two, was lady in waiting to Catherine of Aragon, the incumbent Queen. She herself died only a few years later in 1529, having expended her energies in the meanwhile in ensuring, so far as she was able, a satisfactory future for her children. She was aided in this by Sir Thomas who had left all his land and belongings to her and her children. She also had wealth in her own right.

Included in her possessions was Nazeing Wood. This she had leased in 1527 from Robert, the Abbott of Waltham. This was but two years before her own death and after Katherine had married Lord Borough.

This is the only mention, in the records we have perused, of Parr property in Nazeing. But it is unequivocally merely a tract of woodland with no mention of a house attached - myths arise from small beginnings. It is I am afraid too fanciful a conjecture that Henry met Katherine in these woods, but a stone's throw from his hunting lodge at Green Mead.

Quite why Maud acquired the wood, the site of Nazeing Common, is not recorded. The most likely explanation is purely as an investment: coppicing and sale of the timber brought in an income. Her possession of it continues to feature in indentures, as in an agreement made between Henry VIII and Sir Anthony Denny in 1541, indicating that her lease had continued in spite of her death and the Dissolution. In a further document between Edward VI and Sir Anthony, dated 1547 mention is made of his lands in and around Nazeing, including:

> 'all the lands meadows feeding and pastures situate and being in Nasing aforesaid late in the tenure of the Lady Matilda Parre widow late wife of Thomas Parr Knight deceased.' 2

By this description the original woodland seems to have

been improved somewhat to include land for grazing as well as for coppicing.

Katherine spent her early years at court and was fortunate to receive a humanist education thanks to her mother and other enlightened women at court. In her early teens she was wedded to Lord Borough of Gainsborough, a rich but elderly widower. He died in 1528 and she subsequently married another widower, Lord Latimer. Aged forty, he had large estates in the North and was fairly active politically, ably assisted by Katherine who at one stage had to intercede with the king on his behalf. He died in 1543, the same year she became Queen of England by marrying Henry. The king had become impressed by her political and religious maturity and felt that he could trust her. She was Queen for some three and a half years. When Henry went to war in France she was left as regent and managed affairs to fairly general satisfaction. Shortly after Henry's death in 1547 she married Thomas Seymour a rollicking admiral, brother of Edward the Earl of Somerset and the Protector. Perhaps she married Thomas in the hopes of having a little gaiety in life following her heavy responsibilities. But alas this was not to be. She died not long after childbirth of puerperal sepsis. Her ghost supposedly still visits Sudely Castle the place of her death and burial.

Ann Parr married William Herbert, later the Earl of Pembroke. She was one of the ladies in waiting to Jane Seymour the mother of Edward VI and subsequently to her sister Katherine.

William married Anne the daughter of Henry Bourchier, Earl of Essex who owned Baas Manor in Broxbourne where he is reputed to have died following a fall from his horse. William and Anne lived there, but not happily. William, being suspicious of the parentage of his children moved out, leaving his wife in penury.[3] Fortunately Baas Manor survived even if the hapless Anne did not and is now the home of David and Mary Parsons and a haven of beauty and tranquility.

William became a favourite of King Henry VIII and served him with distinction, thereby earning himself the title of the Earl of Essex, that title of his late father in law which had subsequently been briefly usurped by Thomas Cromwell the king's chancellor before that gentleman's precipitate demise. Following Henry's death William's career petered out. He died in 1571.

1 Agnes Strickland. *Lives of the Queens of England*,vol 3 p175 et sec

2 Wake 167

3 *Wormley in Hertfordshire.* Dorothy Busby

Chapter 6

The Dennys

The dissolution of the monasteries by command of Henry VIII caused considerable upheaval amongst these enclosed orders. Waltham Abbey surrendered in 1540, the last to do so, possibly reflecting Henry's penchant for it. The large estate appertaining to the monastery was put into the immediate charge of Thomas Cromwell, Chancellor to the king, who had been substantially responsible for the pillage of the churches. But he became too greedy and his financial acquisitions led to the loss of his office and his head that same year. These properties then reverted to the crown.

Following this closure the monks were pensioned off and their monastic buildings were probably dismembered at this time - the stone being re-used for other building and the lead from the roofs turned into grapeshot for the navy, being melted by bonfires of the timbers.

Nazeing Bury, which until this time had been one of many properties in the ownership of the abbey, likewise came into the possession of the crown which also took over the duties of the lord of the manor. These duties, which we have been able to glimpse through some of the quoted indentures, encompassed estate management, collection of rents and the resolution of petty criminality. These two functions depended on the manorial courts presided over by the lord or his deputy; the estates and duties were acquired by Anthony Denny.

Anthony Denny was born in nearby Cheshunt in 1501, the son of Sir Edmond, King's Remembrancer to Henry VII and a Baron of the Exchequer. His mother, Mary Troutbeck, was cousin to two of Henry VIII's Queens, Anne Boleyn and Catherine Howard. He was educated at St. Paul's school and

Cambridge after which he entered the diplomatic service around the age of twenty.[1] He must have been a man of singular presence and capability, receiving as he did many offices of the King including that of King's Remembrancer, thus following in his father's footsteps, Keeper of St. James's Park, Hatfield and of the Royal Household. In 1538 he was made a Privy Councillor and became a confidant of the King, to the extent of confiding to him later the news that he was dying. He had over the years acquired various estates. The King being chronically short of money would grant gifts of land rather than money to those in his debt, the Dissolution giving him ready access to much prime property.

In 1536 Denny was granted the site of Cheshunt Nunnery after its dissolution. In 1539 he was given Harolds Park by John Dudley, Earl of Warwick, quite why goes unrecorded. Dudley was then an up and coming leader of Henry's troops, both on land and at sea. Maybe Harolds Park was a gift from the king which Dudley subsequently swapped with Denny for land elsewhere.

In 1540 Denny acquired various items, especially listed for him in the inventory, from Waltham Abbey. A year later he really came into his own so far as the Waltham estates were concerned, being granted the lease for 31 years of most of the land formerly belonging to Waltham Abbey which included:

1. Waltham Grange, the Manor of the home farm of the Abbey lying to the North of the monastic buildings, the Northlands. This manor, or a previous one on the same site, was the pre-eminent manor in Harold's arrangement of his secular monks of Waltham.

2. Dallance in Waltham Park, that estate previously mentioned which Henry had developed and appointed Denny as its keeper. It lay a mile or so N.E. of the Abbey. Joan and Anthony Denny almost certainly resided there for a while and it remained the Denny home, Joan died there, as later did their son Henry.

3. 'the Manor of Nasynge alias Nasingbury, a close called Quenemead and all lands in Nasing lately in the hands of Matilda Parre, rectory of Nasynge andtithes, lately devised to Tho. Cromwell Kt. late of Essex.' All for an annual payment of £127.10. 6. [2]

Excepted was the timber of the vicarage, a pasture at Innynge's, the rents of tenants and the profits of the courts and leets, all of which were presumably retained by the crown.

This lease marks the termination of the manorial rights by the Abbey in favour of secular control by Anthony Denny, as aforementioned, and whose family retained ownership of most of Nazeing, as well as Waltham Abbey, for the next one hundred years and more.

He also acquired the lease of a thousand acres of land around St. Albans, land which ultimately came into his possession.

Prior to this in 1538 he had married Joan Champernowne, a lady says Morant, 'of great parts and beauty,' by whom he had five sons and four daughters including Henry and Edward. Joan was another of the 'humanist' ladies at Henry VIII's court and a friend and ally of Katherine Parr.

In 1544 Anthony Denny was knighted by the King at Boulogne-Sur -Mer, during one of Henry VIII's trips to France, as an appreciation of his services. These were also well regarded by many others, Anthony Denny acting as a useful means of access to the King. Besides these duties he had under his intermittent care Elizabeth the future Queen, both at Cheshunt and at Hatfield, then a royal palace. He was an executor of the King's will and an appointed guardian of the boy King Edward VI. Intermittently he served as a soldier and in 1549 went with Edward Seymour, Duke of Somerset, and William Parr, Katherine's brother and now the Earl of Essex, to quell Ketts' rebellion in Norfolk. He died that same year and was buried in St. Mary's Church, Cheshunt. Lady Joan who died in 1553 was also buried there but no monument to either has been found.

There is no evidence that Sir Anthony Denny ever resided at Nazeing Bury.The house continued in occupation by tenant farmers, with use of surrounding lands, meadows and pastures for their crops and their beasts, as already described during John Nankotton's tenure.

In 1544, five years before Sir Anthony's death:

> 'for the sum of £1800 Ralph Sadler acquired the reversion of all that Manor Farm and demesne lands of Nasyng Lands late of Waltham Monastery, [including other lands in Gloucester, London, etc.]
>
> 'and also those lands meadows feedings pastures with the appurtenances in Nasing in the tenure and occupation of Dame Matilda Parr.'[3]

Sir Ralph Sadler, born in 1507, was an affluent courtier well regarded by Henry VIII. He had also been in cahoots with Thomas Cromwell and during the Dissolution had been granted great swathes of property by the chancellor which happened to include the Manor of Nazeing. Following Cromwell's death, as mentioned above, the Nazeing property was leased to Anthony Denny.

But the above quoted reversion seems a strange declaration, Matilda Parr having by this time been dead for fifteen years and, more importantly, Anthony Denny having already been granted the lease of these same lands. Why for £1800 is Sir Ralph granted the reversion since they had by then been re-acquired by the state in the form of the King and granted to Anthony Denny? Probably some intrigue at court is to blame.

A rather nicely preserved book of the Life of Sir Ralph Sadler contains further details of indentures concerning this vacillation of ownership.[4] Whatever the reasons, Sir Ralph briefly became again the possessor of Nazeing Bury.

He was a privy councillor to Henry VIII and was sent on several high state missions to Scotland. On one occasion he was accompanied by William Parr on a venture concerning Mary

Queen of Scots, whose guardian he was, regarding a possible marriage between her and the future king Edward VI. He later built a house, Standon Lordship at Standon, Hertfordshire, where he died in 1587. There is a monument to him in Standon Parish Church.

Whatever the underlying shenanigans had been, the following year, 1545, by payment into the Augmentation fund, that fund set up by Henry to collect the revenue resulting from the Dissolution, Anthony Denny re-established his title to the manor and rectory of Nazeing. This was in the form of a lease for a further 35 years.

In 1553 Edward VI, now aged sixteen, leased the Manor of Nasing, together with other properties, to Johanne Denny, widow, during the minority of her son Henry. No doubt this was as a token of affection of Edward the king for the late Sir Anthony Denny and indeed for Joan his widow.

In the same year Lady Joan was granted outright possession of the Manors of Waltham and Nasying by King Edward VI just before his death. Thus ownership at last, but for his widow and not for Anthony himself, of this great estate which had been granted to the Abbey by Richard nearly four hundred years before. But sadly not for long since Joan herself died later that same year.

She had appointed John Tamworth to act as executor during the minority of her elder son **Henry Denny**, born in 1540. In 1561 at his coming of age, Tamworth released to him this estate at which time he was living at the family home of Dallance aforementioned.

Surviving records suggest that attaining his majority rather went to his head. Already married, he straight away began to divest himself of his inherited property. During the following nine years he had leased out Claverhambury, Hollyfield, one hundred and more cottages, together with dovecotes, barns and orchards and some 20,000 acres.[5] At the end of this spending spree he evidently ceded the remainder of his property to his executors who were perhaps becoming anxious at his spendthrift ways. Even so the following year he revoked this agreement.

His first marriage was to Honora, daughter of William, Lord Gray of Wilton, by whom he had three children: Robert who died young but came briefly into ownership of the Manors after the death of his father in 1573, Anne and finally Edward, born in 1569, who succeeded to ownership in 1576 at the tender age of seven. Following the death of his first wife, Henry married Elizabeth Grey but he died soon after aged only thirty three.

Henry's brother Edward, a much more colourful character, was born in 1547. The younger Edward's uncle, I shall refer to him as **uncle Edward**, married Margaret Edgecombe and became a soldier of fortune in Ireland, that country even then suffering more than its fair share of mercenaries. He sired nine children and for some reason is remembered in Waltham Abbey by a large and impressive memorial depicting himself and his wife with all their children. He died in 1600 but the Denny family continues to this day through his, uncle Edward's, descendants.

Edward Denny, the nephew, was only four when his father Henry died. His mother being also dead he was left as a ward of his uncle Edward. Whether he accompanied him to Ireland is unknown. He later considered his uncle to have squandered some of his inheritances and perhaps this explains why, when in his later years running short of suitable heirs, uncle Edward's children benefited not at all.

Like his grandfather Anthony, Edward attended St.John's College, Cambridge. He married in 1590 Mary, the granddaughter of Lord Burghley, who lived across the river Lea at Theobalds and was at that time the most powerful man in the kingdom as chief minister to Queen Elizabeth. Edward had been knighted the previous year, at the age of twenty, probably at the instigation of his Lordship, thereby making him a more respectable catch for Mary. For residence he was building the Abbey House, adjacent to Waltham Abbey, out of stone from the ruins of the late monastery. Whether Dallance had continued to be his home after his father's death, with or without his uncle, is unclear. He subsequently laid out the grounds on the site of the monastery which now comprise the Abbey Gardens and thus was not entirely penniless.

He became MP for Liskeard and in 1604 for Essex. He was appointed a Commissioner for Sewers for the river Lea, a more important job than it sounds since it was in part concerned with flood relief measures, the resolution of disputes between the bargemen and the millers and probably jurisdiction of the toll bridge and the mill at Broxbourne as well as the revenue therefrom.

For several years from 1598 occur references to court proceedings taken against him by Coke, attorney to Queen Elizabeth, regarding franchises and property rights in Waltham and Nazeing forests. It would appear he had ridden rather roughshod over local rights. He was not finally issued a general pardon until 1626, in which same year he was created the Earl of Norwich.

In 1603 he appears to have been forced to eat humble pie by the commoners. In an edict entitled 'The Decree for the tents [tenants] of Nasing,'6 which was made at the Manor Court of Nasinge, all timber growing on the estates of the copyholders was deemed to belong to them. They were granted free rights 'to lopp, topp, carry away and sell' any timber on their lands. Sir Edward and Dame Mary were debarred from these timber rights although anyone wilfully spoiling the trees or the hedges would suffer forfeit of their estate.

The copyholders were those tenants of lands and dwellings sanctioned by the lord of that manor, their rights being ensured by their names being copied on the court rolls. Hence these rolls contain many details concerning decease of copyholders, their willed successors and so forth. The manor of Nazeing during the 17th century had some where between twenty and forty copyholding tenants.

In order that estates were well run it was in the interests of the lord to have contented tenants, the ethos of the landlords generally being for good husbandry rather than massive profits.[7] But this decree suggests that relations were not altogether amicable between Sir Edward Denny and his copyholders and the latter were flexing their muscles and asserting their rights towards what they perceived as theirs, as for example the timber.

These relations seem to have continued in a state of some tension. In 1623 he took a case to court complaining that an excessive number of sheep had been grazed on the common, which sheep he rounded up and impounded. The copyholders promptly took their revenge by cutting down the pound. He was also in trouble regarding the roads through the forest which were unsatisfactory. But despite requests from the King's Council, the King wishing to hunt across these lands, he neglected to remedy the matter.

Sir Edward Denny was High Sheriff of Hertfordshire, his land in the county being inherited from his grandfather. In 1603 it was in this capacity that he welcomed King James at Royston, at the head of 140 well mounted men, marching south to claim his kingdom and be crowned as King James I. As an acknowledgement of this auspicious event he presented James with a fine and richly accoutred horse, no doubt hoping this would be remembered to his advantage.

The King was accompanied on this journey by James Hay his friend and confidant and Denny's future son in law. It was perhaps as a result of these coincidences that in 1608 he was granted by the king the forge and stable at Waltham, that stabling formerly used by Henry VIII. He was also given the barn, granary, fulling mills and meadows in Waltham. Evidence of this is contained in a most impressive document with illuminated heading and the great seal of King James 1.[8] Edward had obviously inherited his grandfather's knack of making use of royalty.

In 1607 King James exchanged The Palace at Hatfield for Theobalds, the former residence of Lord Burghley, thus giving him a seat in close proximity to Sir Edward Denny and his friend James Hay. This also enabled the Cecils to commence their long and successful ownership and building creativity at Hatfield, which continues to this day.

Edward Denny appears to have been astute or lucky in financial matters. A lot of his money was inherited as was his land. Even though his father had leased or sold various properties his territorial possessions were still considerable comprising most of Nazeing and Waltham together with its various manors and the Forest of Waltham, in all some 10,000 acres and this is excluding his Hertfordshire lands. Thus in an indenture dated 1617 he provided £10,000, a considerable sum in those days, to his granddaughter Ann out of his investments in the East India Company.

Edward and Mary had one daughter, **Honora**, born in 1591. She was, as a result of her father's monetary machinations, considered the richest heiress of her time and in 1607 married the aforementioned James Hay who, apart from titles, received numerous grants of land from King James to extricate him from debt. Neither Honora nor her father were overjoyed at the prospect of James as respectively husband and son-in-law. The

King seemed to be pushing the match with the hope perhaps of the Denny fortune cushioning James's financial casualness. It is said that on one occasion when entertaining his guests he had them all served cold fare, only at the last moment to have this taken away and replaced with something hot. Possibly the Barony of Waltham was given Denny as a sweetener by the king.

As a marriage gift, in 1608 Edward Denny granted to the: 'Right Hon. James Lord Hayeand her Right Hon. Ladye Honor Hay his wife and daughter of Lord Denny of Waltham, all his Manor of Nasinge, Nasing Wood and Harolds Park.'

Harolds Park being that house and land first mentioned in Richard I's edict granting it to the Abbey and subsequently acquired by Sir Anthony Denny . It is sited on the south eastern side of Nazeing Park on the ridge leading south to Waltham Abbey.

Over the following centuries this great estate of Waltham and Nazeing was gradually sold off, being at the same time parcelled into smaller and smaller pieces, which process commenced in 1608 when Edward Denny gifted Nazeing to his daughter.

In 1630 Edward (created the Earl of Norwich in 1626) submitted his 'Pleas of the Forest' to a hearing of the Lord Chief Justice.[9] He certainly kept the courts busy and in this plea he requested the facility of holding the Courts and the administration of justice within the half hundred of Waltham. He also requested the right to have freedom within the parks of Waltham and Harolds Park and permission to enclose them, to appoint his own woodman, to have his animals within the parks and to take his own firewood - this last perhaps a further attempt to get his own back on the commoners.

He supported these claims by producing the charters going

back to that of Richard I and quoting subsequent privileges enjoyed by Abbot Robert at the time of the Dissolution, which rights he argued were also owed to him since he had lawfully been bequeathed these estates through his forbears.

I think it is likely his pleas were granted, at least so far as the courts were concerned, since we have good evidence, as mentioned in the chapter on the Courts, of their continuation. Edward probably wished to take them back under his direct control rather than their relegation to James his son in law as perhaps occured when he granted him Nazeing Bury as a marriage portion. I think it doubtful he re-established his supposed rights in the park and the firewood therein, the commoners would have stood up for their own.

1 *The Worthies of Waltham.* K.N.Bascombe
2 Wake 163
3 Wake 167
4 Ralph Sadlier State Papers. At Hertford R.O.
5 ERO D/DJg M43
6 Ibid
7 Felix Hull. Agriculture & Rural Society. E.R.O.
8 Wake 194
9 Wake 205

Overleaf:
The extended Pegrum Family, photographed at the Bury on the occasion of fiftieth birthday celebrations.

Chapter 7

Back to the House

Whilst its ownership has been changing over the years what has been happening to the fabric of the house and who has been living there?

There is no evidence that those who owned Nazeing Bury ever resided there before the 19th century. It was a useful source of income to its owners, the equivalent of having shares in the stock market. But money was also spent on its upkeep and gradual enlargement, the landlord investing in the structure whilst the tenant was responsible for general maintenance as is spelt out in several indentures. From a study of these it is my belief that from the earliest times the owner - the abbots, followed by the secular ownership of respectively the Dennys, the Jones and the Wakes, rather than the tenant, took responsibility for structural alterations and rebuilding.

The house is set on gravel, some of the little remaining gravel of the Lea Valley basin. A clay substratum begins to encroach in the grounds to the North East. I think it reasonable to presume it is set on the site of that even earlier medieval building extant at the time of King Harold. John Walker has described the layout of the house as it might have been when John Nankotton acquired it - a timbered hall with various extensions heated by an open hearth.

The first ordnance survey map of 1873 depicts the remains of a moat, an inverted U North of the house which confirms the longevity of the site. Several of the old Nazeing houses were also moated although I find it difficult to believe that these moats ever entirely surrounded them. The last remains of this one were filled in just before we arrived in 1960.

The current house has a **timber frame**, the earlier part all of oak. The basic timber 'box framed' construction is some thirty feet in width by eighteen in depth and two storey height, the vertical posts being connected by hefty horizontal timbers. See fig.1. This two bay box is now surmounted by three A frames sitting on tie beams, the cross members of which support 30 foot 7"x 5" clasped side purlins. These are in turn supported by queen posts. Slots exist in the tie beams probably for central crown posts in the original construction, although John Walker thinks it more likely these are reused beams.

These frames support a hipped and gabled roof erected probably when the roof was raised around 1690. The rafters for this have been deeply marked by the joiners, as the working practice then was, in Roman numerals. This to keep track of the timber being prepared and assembled on the ground before erection took place. Workmanship is good and solid. The original hall would have been the core of the house, as described in chapter 2, the venue for daily living and for the Courts. The floor is now stone flagged, laid no doubt on the original mud flooring.

The **chimney stack** is a fairly massive affair in brick, 2 1/4 inch, some 8 by 8 feet at its base narrowing at roof level to 7 by 4 feet. It transmits the flues from inglenook fireplaces in the hall and adjoining room on the ground floor and two flues from adjacent first floor rooms. I think it likely that this was inserted inside the preexisting hall, before there was a first floor ceiling, by Sir Anthony Denny around 1542. A staircase being also inserted around this chimney at the same time. This dating would also fit, see chapter 2, for the installation of the floor above the hall and the adjoining rooms, quite an expensive rebuild.

My reason for this surmise is that he had just been granted a thirty year lease to Nazeing Bury and was at that time almost certainly involved with the revamping of Nazeing Park and the building of the hunting lodges there at the behest of his king,

Henry VIII, see chapter 11, hence he had access to builders and materials. In addition he had the wealth and, being the leaseholder, the financial stimulus to undertake this upgrading. This in turn would enable the continuation of the courts and their resulting revenue which in 1547 amounted to £31 - 18. [op.cit. chapter 4.] The face lift would also have helped to attract a tenant of the necessary calibre to farm the surrounding acres.

A **cellar** underlies the eastern front wing of the house floored with narrow bricks and with a central gully directing water south under the curtilage. The water level rises and falls with the seasons, hence a certain dampness prevails. This cellar would have been used variously for storing wine, coal and other items. I still possess two large slabs of slate, formerly shelving in this cellar. Before the north wing was constructed access would have been direct from the outside by means of the still existing steps. In this cellar our children when young made a snuggery but found it rather unsnug. Walker concedes this may have been Edward Denny's contribution to the structure.

That was its anatomy, now for its **inhabitants.**

The first for whom records exist is George Congreve in the year 1502, as already detailed. George sounds to have been very much in control of the estate which he farmed. He would have been assisted by hired labourers, perhaps inhabiting the house or adjacent tenements, the former villeins and bordars. He was followed by John Nankotton, who no doubt perpetuated the practices of George Congreve and his ilk, assuming he did actually live there. It is possible he acquired the lease in order to sublet the premises whilst continuing his London merchandising business.

The next documented resident is John Ramsey, as we know by the evidence of Ramsey's will written in 1568[1], who might well have been a tenant ever since the1540's improvements. This most informative document relates that he leased Nazeing Bury, which he was able to leave to his son Thomas, from Robert Hall Esq. of Nazeing who was presumably a local factotum or steward acting for Henry Denny, the Lord of the Manor at that time. Hall died in 1581 and was buried at All Saints.

John Ramsey would seem to have been a prosperous farmer possessing milch beasts, four of which he left to his wife along with other live stock. He also owned land and stables at North Weald Bassett which he bequeathed his other son, Jerome.

'To my wife the brass and pewter which she brought to me at marriage, and my best bed of feathers, for her life; after her decease to Joan Campe my daughter.'

He also stipulated his wife should: 'have 1 year's abiding in a chamber over the parlour on the west end of the house which I dwell in. . . and with meat, bread and drink of the best and firewood ready prepared to her hand freely.' His son Thomas was left his goods, plate, jewels and apparel.

John Ramsey died in September 1569, followed three years later by his son Jerome who evidently lacked his father's competence. Being asked on his death bed how he would dispose he replied:

' I know not what is mine to give (a little, God what knows) but that which is mine to give I give to my sister Mary and if I had more I would give her more.'

Because of the rapid population growth during the following decades, life was not easy for those with little or no property. There was also a more general feeling of dissatisfaction amongst the growing number of non-conformists or so called puritans in the community.

1 op.cit. chapter 2. nos 80 & 181

Chapter 8

The Pilgrim Fathers

Consequent to this mood of unease, in early 17th century, a pilgrimage was taking place from Old to New England.

This emigration was triggered by religious and material factors. Land tenure was becoming increasingly difficult, both for the yeoman farmers because of the Enclosures Acts which were depriving them of accessible farming land and for the more lowly peasants because of the whims of their masters and inflation leading to lower real wages. In addition taxes were becoming more than merely punitive. Another considerable cause of complaint to those of a thinking and religious disposition was the demand of Archbishop Laud that his flock should bow to his dictat, the Act of Conformity of 1633. Whilst an increasing number of people wished for freedom to worship in their own way, instead they had to attend the Sunday sermon and endure other imposed rites such as the use of the surplice, the sign of the cross and the use of the ring in baptism. The Anglicans feared the return of Catholic practices and rumours of conflicting prejudices were rife.

All of these factors were operative in Nazeing at this time. Prominent amongst these non-conformists were John Eliot and the Payson brothers, all of whom were Cambridge graduates and had probably come under the influence there of Thomas Hooker a fellow of Emmanuel College and an inspiring member of this sect.

Lawrence Payson married Joane Webb in 1605. They were the parents of **Giles and Edward Payson** and possibly resident at Nazeing Bury. As an aside, in 1607 Lawrence was burgled of some jewellery from his house, by Richard Burbry, a labourer of Nazeing who was sentenced to be hung for this

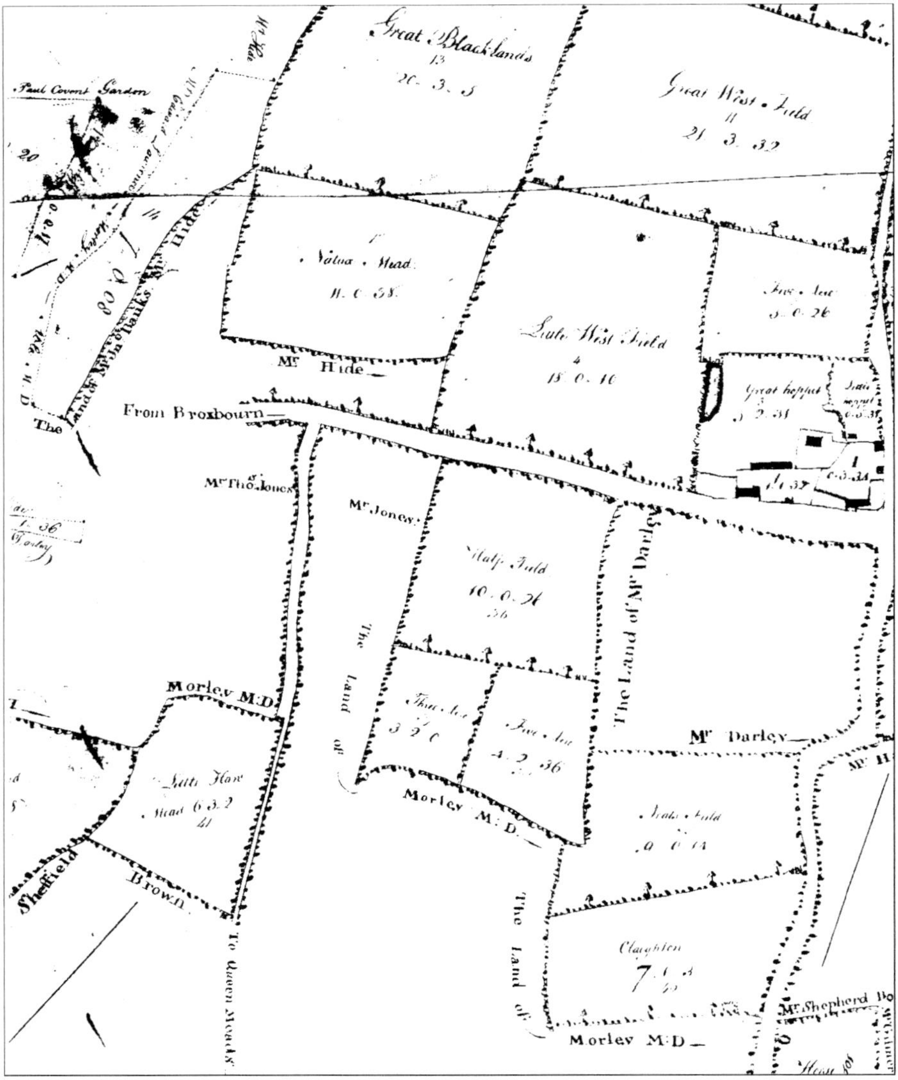
Great Blacklands
Paul Covent Garden
Great West Field
Little West Field
Five Acre
Great hoppet
Mr Hide
From Broxbourn
The Land of Mr Jno Banks
Mr Thos Jones
Mr Jones
Half Field
The Land of Mr Darley
Mr Darley
The Land of
Morley M:D
Little Haw Mead
Sheffield
Brown
To Queen Meads
Claughton
Mr Shepherd

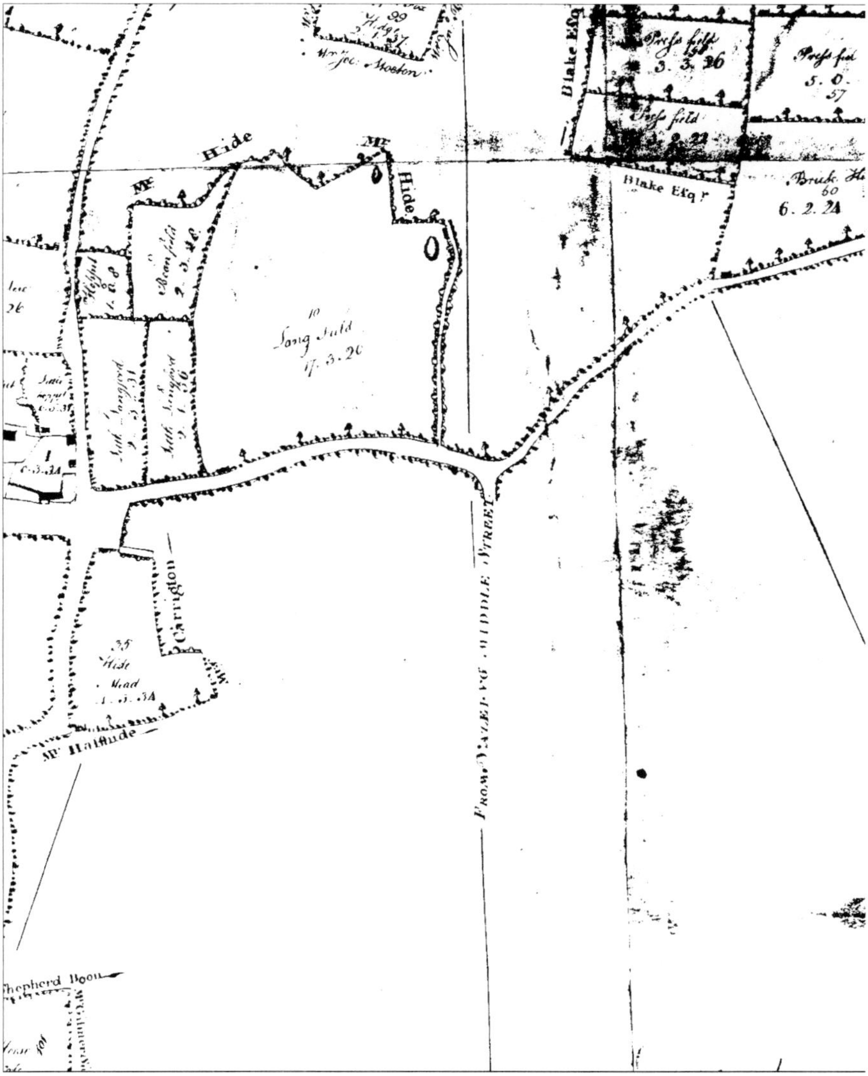

Map dated 1767 commissioned by Sir William Wake

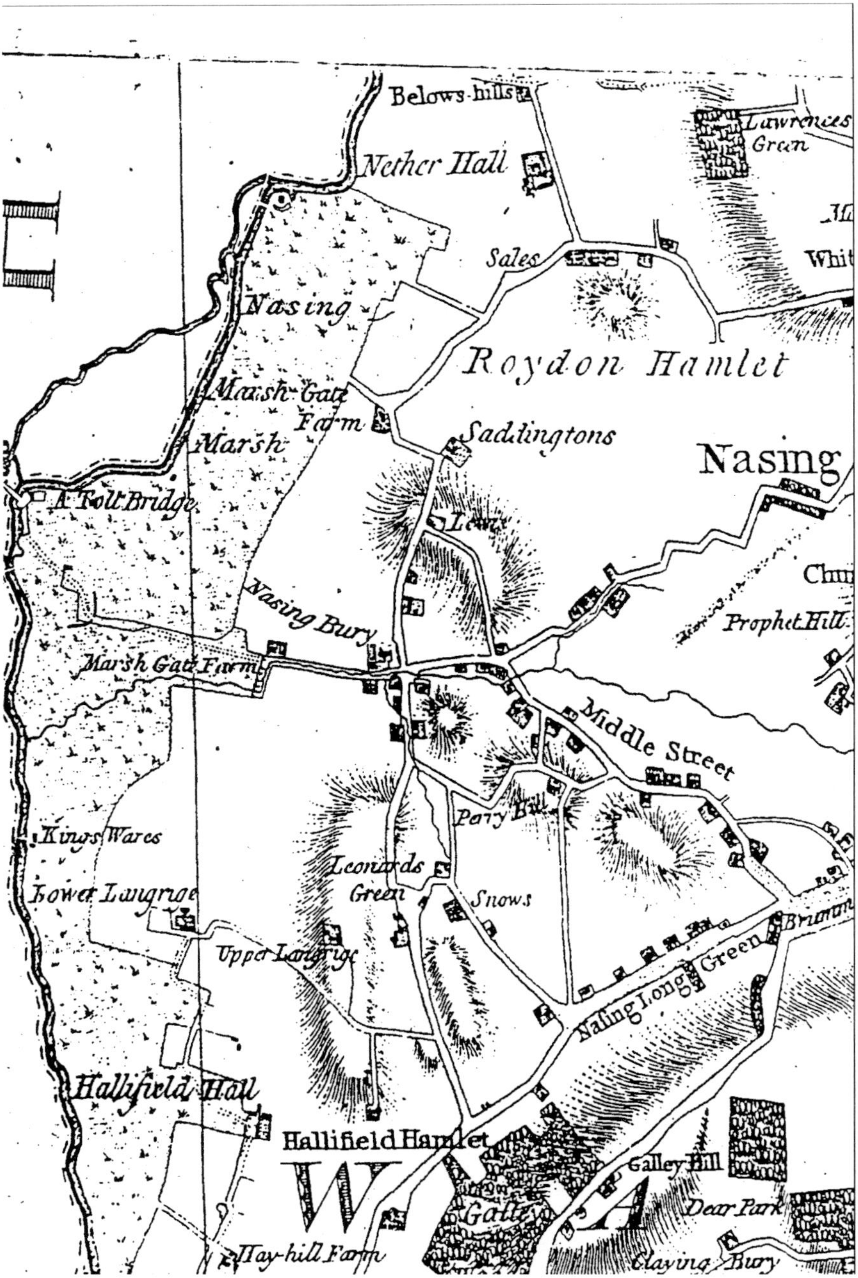

Map dated 1774 by J Chapman & P Andre

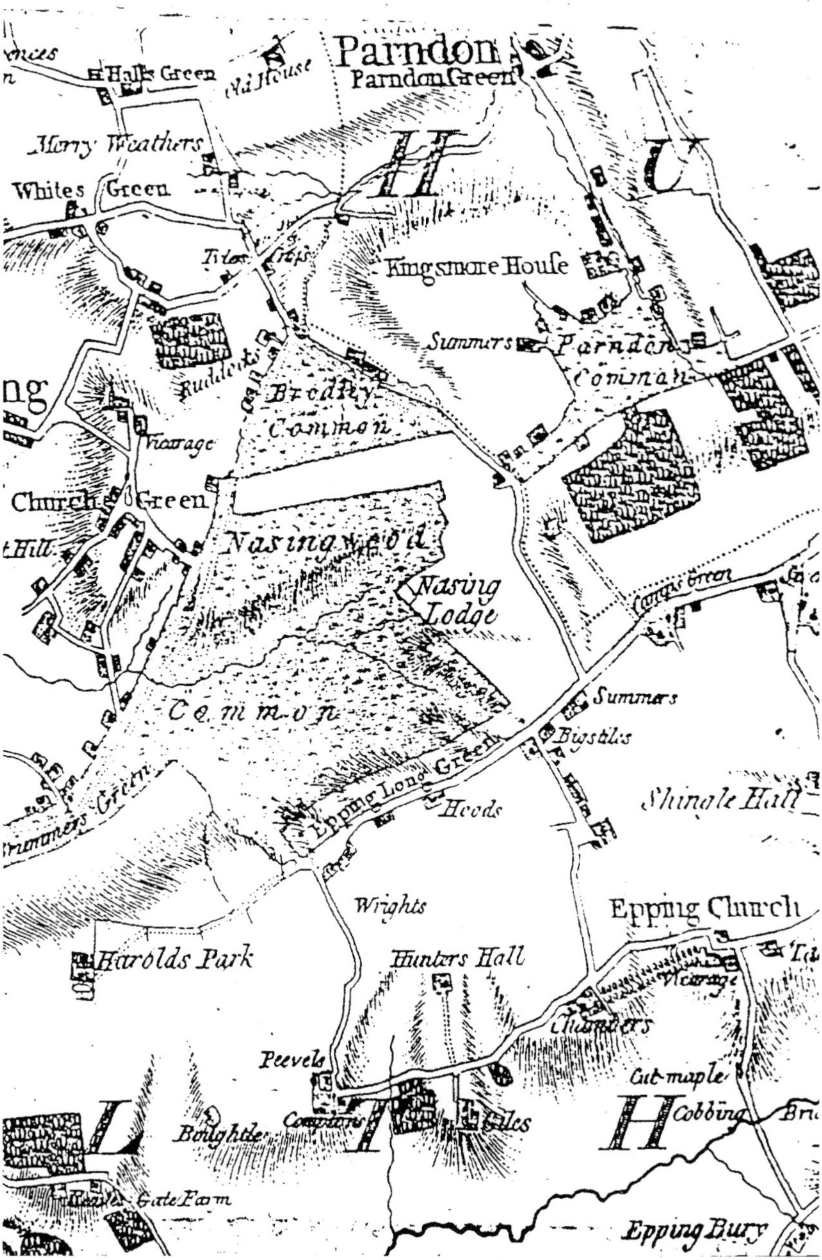
Parrndon
Parndon Green
Halls Green
Old House
Merry Weathers
Whites Green
Kingsmore House
Summers
Parndon Common
Bredley Common
Vicarage
Church Green
Nasingwood
Nasing Lodge
Common
Summers
Bigstiles
Epping Long Green
Hoods
Shingle Hall
Wrights
Epping Church
Harolds Park
Hunters Hall
Vicarage
Chambers
Peevels
Cut maple
Cobbing
Gate Farm
Epping Bury

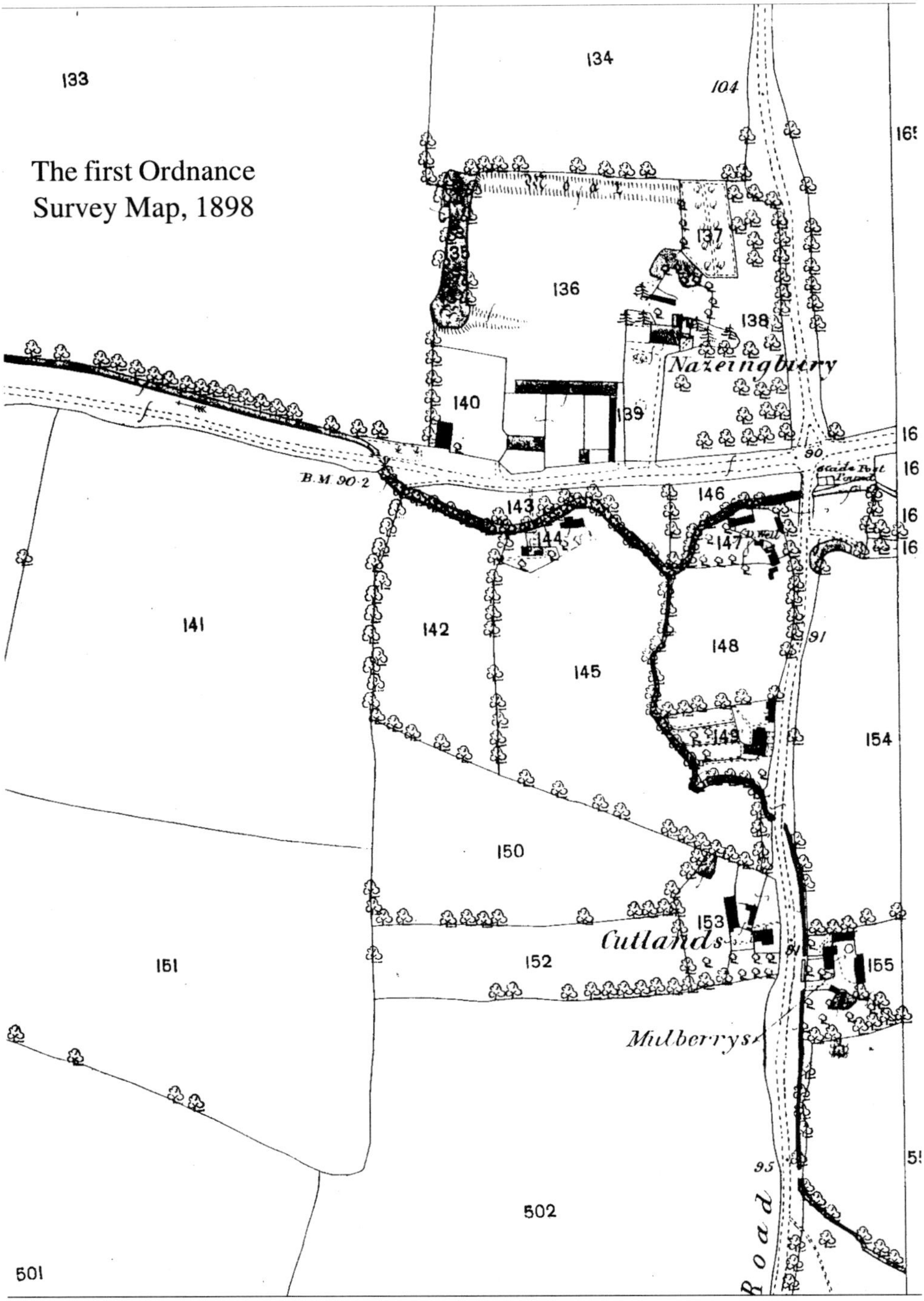

The first Ordnance Survey Map, 1898

felony, this being his second offence.[1] Giles was born in 1609 and Edward in 1613. It is certain that a 'John Pason' was resident at the Berri in 1637.[2]

John Eliot was born in 1603 at Widford and his parents moved to Nazeing in 1608, several members of the family featuring in the All Saints register.

A possibility therefore is that the young students, Giles and Edward Payson and the slightly senior John Eliot may have conversed together at Nazeing Bury.

Following his undergraduate years at Cambridge and his ordination Eliot spent some four years in the community at The Cuckoos in Little Baddow, again under the aegis of Thomas Hooker. This gathering of non conformists formed one of the many movements of the time undermining conformity. It was here that much of the planning for their forthcoming work in the New World took place. Situated just outside Chelmsford, its spirit and historical associations are still extant.

Hooker himself sailed to America in 1633, settling in Newtown (now Cambridge) not far from Boston. In the following years he achieved much by his writing and preaching towards the foundation of the United States of America.

John Eliot preceded him in 1630, sailing aboard the Arbella with his brother Philip in the company of John Winthrop, destined to be governor of the new colony in Massachusetts. Also on this ship, the flagship of the Dorchester company who were pioneering the settling of New England, was George Phillips, also a Cambridge graduate, a non-conformist minister whose granddaughter married Edward Payson's son.

John Eliot quickly became a founder member of the non conformist church in Roxbury sited just outside what is now Boston, Massachusetts. He was joined there six years later by Giles and Edward Payson who had sailed out aboard the Hopewell with several others from Nazeing including 'Georg Homes', listed in the parish register as having been baptised in

1592. He was accompanied by his wife Deborah and daughter Lydia.[3]

This site, which had been a bare wilderness, became the focal point for most of the Nazeing New Englanders. In 1632 Eliot's was the first wedding in the new church to Hannah Mumford whom he had first met at Little Baddow. His life's work was to bring Christianity as well as European farming and building methods to the indigenous Indian peoples. He also translated the Bible and other works into the Algonquin language, overcoming great difficulties since they had no written language and founded many schools for them in the surrounding areas. In addition he concerned himself with the further education of the English settlers and enabled their integration with the Indians at Harvard which was beginning to be built even then.[4]

Tragically all his labours were nearly undone in 1675 when a nearby Indian chieftain led an uprising against the settlers causing considerable mayhem which took Eliot and his followers some ten years to rebuild. He died, aged eighty six in 1690. There is a monument to him at the First Church of Roxbury.

Two generations later in Boston another Edward Payson married Thankful Holmes, the granddaughter of George.

Apart from those mentioned above it is thought that some thirty eight others also emigrated from Nazeing and more from Waltham Abbey to America. A plaque in their memory is in the church. The full list as quoted by Collingwood, culled from W. Winters in *Memorials of the Pilgrim Fathers*, includes the following:

Adams, Brevitt, Camp, Clarke, Curtis, Eliot, Gore, Graves, Home, King, Morris, Payson, Peacock, Pegram, Ruggles, Shelley and Uffett.

The majority of these names occur in the church register and had offspring or parents in the village. Some were single young men, some had wives and children, most were devout Puritans. All were prepared to undergo very considerable discomfort, firstly at sea and then on land, in pursuit of freedom and idealism. The ship Planter for example took six months to sail from London to Boston in 1636. To qualify for these pilgrimages all had to produce certificates, signed by a minister and a J.P. affirming that they had taken the oath of allegiance.

The varied skills of these men and women would undoubtedly have been put to full use in their pioneering way of life.

Throughout this 20th century a pilgrimage has been taking place in the reverse direction. Descendants of those who made the first journey, no doubt conscious of the hardships their forebears underwent and themselves leading a much more sheltered life, come back from America to trace their origins in Nazeing, visiting All Saints Church and other places.

I have a letter from Charlotte Webb, then residing at Broxbourne, recalling meeting a Mr. and Mrs Payson who had come over from Boston in 1962 to revisit the village of Nazeing and Nazeing Bury from whence their ancestors had emigrated. An earlier Webb had married one of the first recorded Paysons.

Earlier this year, 1966, I met an American couple at the church who were descended from the Curtis's, also former Bury residents, so was able to show them the house, as I have again recently. Postal enquiries to the Vicarage continue to crop up, a recent one enquiring of the many Harknetts, well established here in previous centuries. Another from a Virginia Butler contained the interesting information mentioned earlier regarding her forbear George Holmes.

1 ERO Winters op.cit. Perhaps from Nazeing Bury (?)

2 Nazeing Parish Records

3 George Holmes of Roxbury, Mass. and his descendants

4 *Thomas Hooker*. Deryck Collingwood

The River Lea near Broxbourne Bridge

Chapter 9

The Earls of Carlisle

The year 1603 was that in which Sir Edward Denny was presented with the decree devised by his tenants demanding their rights to the timber on their estates. This same year marked the death of Elizabeth and the accession of James I. The Tudor court was replaced by the Stuart. Edward Denny bridged these eras. He was married to Mary, granddaughter of Lord Burghley, who had been chief minister to Queen Elizabeth, in whose reign Denny had spent the first thirty years of his life. He welcomed the Stuart dynasty in the form of James I and received several favours from him including a barony. His daughter Honora married James, the first Earl of Carlisle in 1607.

James Hay continued to be occupied by court affairs and unlike his father in law was not conversant with the state of the manor. The couple had two children, Ann and James. Sadly, their mother Honora died of a miscarriage brought on by shock, aged only twenty three, in 1614. She was attacked by a thief whilst driving in her coach late one night down Ludgate Hill.[1] Ann, her daughter, did not live long enough to enjoy her grandfather's inheritance.

In spite of his extravagances James was well respected at court and sent on many diplomatic missions, being in his time the ambassador to Paris, Madrid, Venice and Germany. He never resided in his Nazeing estates, the marriage gift of Lord Denny. In 1615 he was created Baron Hay of Sawley in the county of York and in 1618 made Viscount Doncaster. This followed his second marriage to Lucy Percy in 1617. She was a daughter of Lord Percy of Northumberland, another reluctant father in law. Lucy was a wit and a beauty and also a success at court in her own right, quite apart from being a confidante of Henrietta, Queen to Charles I who had succeeded his father in 1625. This association was no doubt useful to James in his dealings with his new monarch. She continued various activities of a political nature long after the death of her husband, for which she was briefly imprisoned in the tower and even threatened with the rack. Her portrait, painted by Van Dyke, hangs at Petworth where she is buried, having died of apoplexy in her early sixties.

Before this, whilst James 1 was still on the throne, he further honoured his favoured courtier by creating him Earl of Carlisle in 1622, a title derived from the island of that name, before being changed to Barbados. There is still an inlet there known as Carlisle Bay. In 1627 James Hay was made Lord Proprietor of the island by Charles 1. He probably never visited but participated in supervising its affairs through intermediaries in London. The expatriate landowners made their money from crops such as tobacco, cotton, indigo or sugar, depending on the vagaries of the London market. His hopes of its repaying some of his many debts were thwarted by the trustees on Barbados.[2] His son, who continued to receive income from the island, spent some time there during the Protectorate, as did several members of the opposing factions in an attempt to distance themselves from the nastiness of war.

In 1622 James devised his will, awakened perhaps to his paternal duties by increasing eminence. To his son, amongst other things he conveyed:

'the Manor and demesnes of Nasing and Nasingberry. Harold's Park and Greene Mead and Nasingwood. And all those demesne hamlets of the said Manor of Nasing commonly called Nasingberry.'

In the event of the demise of his son they were to be free for the use of his son's wife Lady Margaret during the term of her natural life.[3] James died in 1636, aged only 56, at his house at Whitehall in London from whence he was taken for burial at St. Pauls.

Lord Denny, who outlived his son in law James by a year, was for many years before his death exercised by the problem of who should succeed to his still quite considerable estates, especially as these were rather rapidly being diminished by James. It was probably for this reason that as early as 1617, three years after the death of his daughter Honora, that 'the Manors of Nasinge and Nasingbury,'[4] having initially been put in the care of trustees, were left to James and after to the heir of his wife Lady Honora in other words to his grandson. These properties having already been given to James and Honora as a marriage settlement, Lord Denny was presumably endeavouring to ensure an interest for his grandson.

As a child it seems probable that **James Junior** spent a lot of his time with his grandfather at the Abbey House, Waltham. He cannot have been more than six or so when his mother died thus giving his father even less reason to stay home.

In his youth he did a bit of soldiering in Germany as Colonel of a regiment of foot. This would have been on a mercenary basis during the Thirty Years War. In 1631, home from these wars, he married Margaret, the daughter of Francis the Fourth Earl of Bedford.

The Fourth Earl was quite a power in the land. That same year of 1631 he had just completed the building of Covent Garden designed by Inigo Jones. He later participated, in spite of local opposition, in draining the fens, in order to create more farmland. In the run up to the Protectorate he opposed the king and in 1641 the year of his death, endeavoured to mediate between King Charles I and Parliament. He begat through his wife Catherine, the daughter of Lord Chandos, several children, who included as well as Margaret, William and Edward. Another daughter Elizabeth married Henry, the younger and brighter surviving son of Oliver Cromwell.

The marriage of James and Margaret was probably a satisfactory one, but 'without living male of his body begotten on the body of the said Lady Margaret,' as Lord Edward Denny's will quaintly expresses it. Neither were there any daughters. James became the Second Earl of Carlisle in 1636 on the death of his father. So when Denny wrote his will in that year, shortly before his own death at the age of sixty seven the following year, he had to do a bit of searching for successors. His own wife was made his only executrix, so long as she continued 'sole and unmarried.' She died, still sole, the following year. The only likely candidate for an heir was Denny's nephew George, the son of his sister Ann who was married to George Goring. Otherwise there was no possible family continuity after the death of Denny's childless grandson, James and he had no wish to let his cousins by uncle Edward in on the act. I shall return to nephew George in the next chapter.

In this will Denny left to his grandson James his choice of: 'best houses and manors. and on his, James', death without issue these were to be passed to my beloved nephew George Lord Goring.'

He makes the point in this document that for want of heirs on James part : 'the same should go to such as I appoint.'

The site of the late dissolved monastery and the surrounding lands were to go towards paying his [Denny's] debts and legacies. These assets were thought to be worth something of the order of £1000 p.a.

Perusing the following rather complex legal documents it would appear that these intents of Lord Edward Denny were largely fulfilled.

Both he and his wife were buried in a family vault in Waltham Abbey, not far from the opulent tomb of his uncle.

There is also in the Abbey a floor memorial to Henry Austen, 'Servant to the Rt.Hon.James Earle of Carlisle and Gentleman of his Horse who departed this life 6 of November 1638.' A nice gesture I think by the younger James.

The movements of James and his childless wife Margaret before his grandfather's death are unclear. They were married in 1631 and in 1637 are known to have had a house 'against New Inne Gate' in Waltham Abbey.[5] They may well have lived there since early in their marriage, this being in proximity to Lord Denny, James' grandfather and benefactor. So far as other property was concerned they had been jointly left the manors of Nazeing and Harolds Park as well as Green Mead, Nazeing Lodge and Nazeing Wood. This Nazeing package constituted the chief remaining asset of the Denny fortune, the Waltham estates having been diminished but not evidently abolished by the paying off of Denny's creditors.

In 1646 James and Margaret acquired the lease of Nazeing Wood Grove from a William and Elizabeth Alexander of Roydon,[6] sale of the underwoods still hopefully proving profitable, a harkback to Maud Parr's lease of Nazeing Wood. This suggests they were not too far away which is confirmed by documents from another source on which I elaborate more fully in the later chapter on Nazeing Park.

Nazeing Grove was a wooded area of several acres sited to the north east of the church. Some living oaks still guard the perimeter as do the remains of several more. It was extant from at least 1542 at which time it was enfenced together with Nazeing Wood.

Lord Denny was dead before Charles 1 started waging his long, acrimonious and ultimately fatal battle with Parliament.

This was to result in the polarisation of many citizens to the Royalist or Parliamentarian cause and ultimately to do battle with each other.

James, with or without his wife, spent some years of this Civil War in Barbados, to which he had established his hereditary right as of his father, not returning until 1651. He had perhaps experienced enough of war as a youth in Germany. He may also have been in some doubt as to whose cause to support. His father had been a king's man, although he had died before open discord broke out. His uncle, George Goring, was also a thorough going Royalist as was George's son. But James' father-in-law was active on the Parliamentarian side as was Margaret's brother William, who became the Fifth Earl of Bedford in 1641. Brother William was another dynamic character like his father. At the start of the Civil War he was in command of a troop of Parliamentarian horse, hence in direct opposition to George Goring although I do not think they ever actually met on the field of battle. He later vacillated to the king's side and then back again to Parliament.

In 1643 James, in common with several other erstwhile Royalists in Nazeing, including Sir Francis Swift of Harolds Park, were declared delinquents and suffered sequestration of some of their land. During the 1650's James endeavoured to remain solvent by juggling his remaining securities. Given the problems of his charming but improvident father this would have been difficult enough in normal times but, England having been at war with itself on and off for the past ten years made it doubly so. During these Protectorate years things were still uncertain for former Royalists. James still seems to have had a stake in at least some of the Waltham properties which he now proceeds to dispose of including Claverhambury Manor, assuring Lord Goring, perhaps with tongue in cheek, that this shall not lessen his eventual rights to them. His brother-in-law William, Earl of Bedford, adds respectability as a testator to some of these goings on.

In 1659 a final agreement is made between James and Edward Russell, his brother-in-law, younger brother of William, granting to the latter:

'the Manno of Nasing, Nasingbury with 15 messuages and cottages 200 acres of land 160 acres of meadow 800 acres of pasture 80 acres of wood 100 acres of furze and heath 80 acres of fresh marsh.'

For this Edward was to pay James £1700. Nasingbury thus would appear capable of survival as a self contained unit and it appears very likely that Edward Russell dwelt there until around 1671.7

In 1660, himself approaching sixty years of age and in the year of his own death, James makes his will, a carefully crafted document.

He requests burial next to his grandfather, Edward, the Earl of Norwich, an indication of his affection for him. He abides with the requests made by his grandfather in his indentures of thirty years previous so far as he is able, but so much of the inheritance has become encumbered.

To his trustees, who included his brother-in-law William the Earl of Bedford, he devises all his English lands, (except the manor of Sawley) but including Harolds Park and if necessary Sewardstone Manor, to pay his debts.

He confirms that the manor and rectory of Nasing together with Nasing Lodge and 100 acres of common called Nasing Wood are all to pass to Edward his brother-in-law, which he had sold to him the previous year.

His wife Margaret is appointed sole executor and is left all his plate, jewels and household chattels. For this he requests that she:

'does have at her death out of my best goods and household stuff two of ye best rooms furnished at Greene Mead Lodge, for my godsonne Edward Russell.'

This godson being the eldest son, the others being James and Francis, of Edward his brother-in-law.

His appointed trustees again including the indispensable William, are requested to oversee his will and in case his dear wife should refuse to undertake the trouble are requested to act in her place.[8]

These are the wishes of a man of substance, at least in his own eyes, even though the creditors have already gathered. Green Mead, the origins of which are detailed in chapter 11, seems important to him, perhaps because his nephew Edward has expressed an affection for it. This will certainly confirms James' knowledge of local topography.

Margaret, the Countess of Carlisle, died in 1676 and was buried at Chenies in Buckinghamshire, a country seat of the Bedfords. Prior to that event she acquired two more husbands: she first became the fifth, and last, wife of Edward, Earl of Manchester, being married to him at St. Martin-in-the-Fields in 1667. Earlier in his life during the Civil War he had played an active part in the prosecution of the war on the Parliamentarian side. General of the Eastern armies, together with Fairfax and Cromwell, he participated in the defeat of the Royalist armies at Marston Moor, that battle which George Goring on the opposing side had nearly helped to win. He became disenchanted with Cromwell's rather forceful conduct of affairs and retired from public life until the restoration, which event he welcomed. He was reinstated as chancellor of Cambridge University and as a lord-lieutenant, thus hopefully bringing Margaret at least some material comfort. He died in 1671 following which she married Robert Rich, the fifth Earl of Warwick. Following the death of James, her first husband, she became the lord of the manor presiding, nominally, over some of the Nazeing Courts.

1 K N Bascombe. *Worthies of Waltham*

2 Hilary Beckles *A History of Barbados*

3 Wake 213

4 This may be a reference to 'Great' and 'Little' Nazeing Bury

5 ERO Winters ibid

6 Wake 214

7 Wake 226. In the E R O is a microfilm of the hearth taxes. Listed under Nazeing is a reference to Edward Russell occupying a house of 10 hearths which might well apply to Nazeing Bury.

8 Wake 227

Old oak beams in the attic, below showing the carpenter's mark

Chapter 10

The Goring Connection

George Goring, married to Lord Edward Denny's sister Ann, resided at Hurstpierpoint in Sussex and was evidently an influential man. Leastwise he enabled his son **George Goring**, who was born in 1583, to have a Cambridge education, after which he became attached to Queen Elizabeth's court, entitled a 'Gentleman pensioner', or retainer, of the Queen.

Following Elizabeth's death, George continued his career at the court of James I who enjoyed his wit and company, knighting him in 1608.

George subsequently accompanied Prince Charles, James' heir apparent, to Spain, helping to negotiate Charles' marriage to Henrietta Maria daughter of Henri IV of France, for which service he was created Baron Goring of Hurstpierpoint and made the future queen's Master of Horse. But in spite of these dispensations he was already financially overstretched. Thus in 1633 he was compelled to negotiate a loan of £20,000 from Isaac Jones whose story continues in chapter 12.

Charles I after he became king involved George in several schemes to try to enlarge the state coffers, there being an endemic shortage of money on both their parts. Some of these ventures such as the tobacco monopoly, granted in 1636, and tavern licensing were to their mutual pecuniary advantage, but the ending of these concessions by order of Parliament in the 1640's saw the end of George's days of wealth.

During these increasingly bitter days of struggle between king and parliament, culminating in the Civil War, George acted for the king. He accompanied Henrietta the Queen to Holland in 1642 in an attempt to raise money for the royal cause and in 1644 pleaded help for King Charles I from Cardinal Mazarin of France, not that much help was forthcoming. He was nevertheless created the Earl of Norwich by the king, that title of his late uncle Lord Edward Denny. But Parliament took exception to all this activity and impeached him at which he made off abroad again.

On his return to England in 1647 George, rather by chance, was elected general of the Kentish cavaliers but was defeated by Fairfax, the general in command of the Parliamentarian forces, at Maidstone. Subsequently in another setback he was beseiged at Colchester, forced to surrender and imprisoned at Windsor Castle. Being put on trial by the rather summary Parliamentarian court of justice he was sentenced to death for these various considered misdemeanors but reprieved by the casting vote of the Speaker of the House.

In 1649 George's liege, King Charles I, was executed following a brief trial under the supervision of Oliver Cromwell. George subsequently rather self sacrificially threw in his lot with Charles' son, the young prince. Surprisingly he again managed to cross the channel to join the future Charles II who finally succeeded in 1660, ten long years after the death of his father, in obtaining his crown. This led to improvement in George's lot since he was appointed captain of the king's guard but he never recovered his financial losses, many of which had been incurred on the king's behalf. The king was not mean but whilst in exile he had no money and on his restoration he did not command as much as he would have liked.

George married Mary Nevill, the daughter of the sixth Lord Abergaveney, who died in 1648, but by whom he had six children including another George.

Those are the bare bones of George Goring's public life. So far as his relevance to Nazeing is concerned the facts are as follows. His name first appears in the Wake papers in 1635 when James, the first Earl of Carlisle, whose contemporary he was, leases him some properties including Nasingberry for a 'competent sum.'[1] The two would have been well acquainted by virtue of their court and family connections including Lord Denny, George's uncle and no doubt James' new wife Lucy.This was the time of George Goring's financial peak, thus a useful man for James to know despite his aforementioned debt to Isaac Jones. He would have been conversant with James' financial stringencies and therefore perhaps happy to help him out for reasons of kinship, being no doubt also already privy to his eventual intended inheritance from his uncle.There is no evidence of his ever having resided at Nazeing Bury or other local properties. By his 1635 lease he would have acquired some temporary rights, his pecuniary advantage coming from the tenant, at that time probably John Payson related to the pilgrim Paysons. He would appear to have been over optimistic regarding the income from these outlays.

When in 1636 Lord Denny wrote his will he requested his nephew George to oversee it.[2] No doubt apart from family ties he was also impressed by George's apparent competence in the business world. George's reward for this was to be, assuming as seemed likely that the younger James was going to die childless, the residue of the Manors of Waltham, for some of which he had already taken the lease.

In 1641 Richard, the Earl of Cork and Lord High Treasurer of the Realm of Ireland paid a 'competent' sum for the lease of lands formerly owned by James, the Earl of Carlisle, including the manors of Nasing, Naseingberry and Waltham and the rectory of Nasing together with the vicarage. This payment was to George, Lord Goring, who currently owned the lease. This would have extricated him from a financial hole, but somehow, later that same year, he repaid this mortgage. Such an unlikely transaction arose because Richard Boyle, the said Earl, was George's son's father-in-law.

George, the Earl of Norwich, died in 1663 at Brentford, by which time his eldest son George had predeceased him. This left his second son Charles to inherit the mantle of the Earl of Norwich and, together with his sisters, the remnants such as they were, of the Waltham and Nazeing estates.

George Goring Junior, born in 1608, married in 1629 Lettice the daughter of Richard Boyle. He inherited his father's ability to charm kings and was one of the most brilliant and prodigal of Charles I's younger courtiers. But his extravagant mode of living, which included gaming and drinking, meant that he frequently also appealed to his father in law for money. Like father, like son! In seeking an alternative source of income he entered the service of the Dutch obtaining command of a troop of horse and foot, but at the siege of Breda he was injured in the ankle.

Returning to England, in 1638 he was appointed governor of Portsmouth at which his father in law congratulated him, as also on his reconciliation with his wife and advised him to abjure immoderate gaming. He later commanded a Scottish regiment on behalf of the Royalists, being involved in shenanigans on behalf of an increasingly insecure King Charles I. As general of his horse he did manage to rout Fairfax at Seacroft Moor but was subsequently captured by Fairfax and incarcerated in the Tower for nine months. On his release he regained his command and in a ding dong battle was beaten by Cromwell at Marston Moor. His final defeat came at Langport at the hands of Fairfax who received the surrender of the king's army. George was a forceful individualist described by Lord Clarendon, the contemporary historian and politician, as having unlimited ambition unrestrained by a respect for justice.

Come the Protectorate he retired to Spain. In expectation of the Restoration he made some half hearted overtures to the future Charles II but died before his father in 1657, hence inherited no properties from him and was thus never a Nazeing landlord.

Charles Goring, son of George, the Earl of Norwich and brother to the other George also participated in the Civil War and fought beside his brother at the indecisive battle of Newbury. He was married to Alice widow of Sir Richard Baker and died aged about sixty only a few years after his father in 1670 leaving a widow but no children.

Of his sisters: Elizabeth was married to William Lord Brereton another Parliamentarian who served as a commander in England and Ireland. He died in 1661 leaving his wife and a daughter Anne.

Mary was married to Sir Drue Deane of Maplestead in Essex and had a son, Anthony.

Diana, whose second marriage was to George Porter who had been a lieutenant-general in the Western Army commanded by his brother in law George Goring. Evidently another not altogether cut out to be a soldier, having been characterised by the latter as being: 'the best company but the worst officer that ever served the king.'

Catherine was the youngest daughter, born around 1620 she was married to, and later divorced from, William Scott of Scotts Hall in Kent.

All now in the latter part of their lives, they were hoping to extract some of the pecuniary advantage promised them by their father. This process was being aided by the acquisitorial tactics of Sir Samuel Jones and his executors who will shortly take centre stage.

But firstly to recapitulate the ownership of Nazeing Bury, so far as this can be ascertained, during the course of the 17th century.

In 1600 it was securely in the hands of Lord Edward Denny who in 1608 gave it as a wedding gift to his daughter Honora and her husband James. They leased it to Lord George Goring in 1635. He in turn in 1641 leased Nazeing Bury and other parcels of land for a few months to the Earl of Cork, the implication being that it was his to dispose of. But come 1659 we have the younger James Hay apparently selling Nazeing Bury, together with quite a lot of land to Edward Russell his brother in law, thus indicating relinquishment of the ownership by George at some stage, although this is subsequently disputed. Nevertheless it appears probable that Edward Russell lived at Nazeing Bury, the first owner so to do, around the 1660's.

What seems certain is that after Margaret's death in 1676, Nazeing Bury and other properties were due to come into the joint ownership of George Goring's daughter in law Alice and his four daughters.

This uncertainty of ownership must have had a detrimental effect on the maintenance of these estates, even though no doubt written into the documents of tenancy would have been a clause concerning upkeep. Unfortunately the names of these tenants are still largely unknown.

1 Wake 206

2 Wake 208

Chapter 11

Nazeing Wood

This stretch of land, Nazeing Wood or Park, more simply known as Nazeing Common or just the Common features in the Wake documents under various other guises. It is relevant to the story of Nazeing Bury since from the Middle Ages until the 17th century the owner was the Lord of the Manor.

David Pracy in his book 'Not a Better Set in the Country', gives a very coherent and interesting account of the history of the Park once formed. The Wake collection and some other documents have provided additional material for this study.

Comprising now some four hundred acres the common is an attractive sweep of countryside, a wide valley terminated at its northern end by Lodge Farm which commands a marvellous vista looking south towards Waltham Abbey. The land is now given over to arable farming, hence its appearance changes with the seasons.

In Richard Coeur de Lion's edict of 1191 mention is made of 'the Great Wood and the Park which is called Harolds Park.' It is probable that this woodland then extended north from the abbey at Waltham to beyond where Lodge Farm now stands. All of this together with the village of Nazeing was granted to the canons of the abbey, that area now known as Nazeing Wood, comprising the N.E. part of the estate. In 1285 at least part of this land was emparked and grazing rights granted to the men of Nazeing by agreement with the canons.

In 1527 Maud Parr was granted by the abbott a lease of the underwoods within Nazeing Wood, the following being a summary:

This indenture was made on November 29 1527 between Robert

Parr in the County of Hertfordshire. It witnesseth that the abbott and canons have sold to Dame Matilda Parr all those underwoods growing within the Nazyng wood, together with all the lopping and topping in this same wood.

It shall be lawfull to Dame Matilda to sell all the underwood and to lop and top all the other woods. This shall be at all seasonable times in the year during the next thirty years. But to the canon and his successors shall remain all manner of oak both old and young, all elms, ashes, beeches, whitethorn and blackthorn.

Excepting a parcel of ground within Nazyng Wood called Grenemedead and all the wood, both young and old, lying within or growing within this same Grenemedead.

For which the abbott at the ensealing of this indenture acknowledges himself satisfied on payment of twenty pounds of lawful money of England. Dame Matilda Parr, acknowledges herself indebted to the abbott for the further sum of £22, which Dame Matilda binds herself to pay to the abbott and his successors in the following manner:

The first payment to be paid at the feast of Saint Michael the archangel in the year of our Lord God 1530, then to pay 20 shillings and in the following years until the sum of £22 be fully paid to the abbott.

IN WITNESS whereof the abbott hath delivered to Matilda Parr part of this indenture sealed with the canons seal of the monastery and signed his name for this date.

Matilda Parr widdow hath sealed the other part of this indenture interchangeably and subscribed her name and hath delivered it to the forsaid abbott and canon for date and deed the day and year aforesaid

signed: Robert Abbott to Waltham Abbey

This document, still well preserved and with most of the original seal of Waltham Abbey, resides at the Essex Record Office.

It was written when the Abbey still owned all the woodland, manors and surrounding land although the status of Green Mead, of which more anon, remains conjectural. It tells us with certainty that Nazeing Wood in the year 1527 really was a wood, which Maud Parr leased for financial gain and the lease contains interesting strictures on the management of this woodland.

Although Maud died in 1529 ownership continues in her name through her executors. It would have expired in 1559.

Green Mead

Evelyn Shirley's book, '*Deer and Deer Parks*' contains a most helpful account of the origins of Green Mead and the development of Nasing Wood. He states there was already an old hunting lodge at Green Mead in 1542, thus explaining Maud's exclusion from that area in 1527 and suggesting King Henry VIII had already by then, and possibly by force majeure, acquired that site. In 1542, by which time this was crown land, a considerable revamping of the area took place, probably with the connivance of Anthony Denny. A 'launde', or open space, was cleared at Green Mead, 'and through this launde the deer will come.' (Shakespeare) This was a costly exercise, a large area must have been involved, trees and their roots needed removing, and on this land a new standing was built. This would have been a fairly simple roofed construct of timber. At the same time a new lodge was built in Nazeing Wood, where now Lodge Farm stands, to harbour the food, horses and other necessaries for the grandees in their standing, Green Mead a short way up the hill, for when they were viewing the hunt.

One hundred years on this simple standing at Green Mead had been upgraded to an inhabited lodge of several rooms, perhaps at the instigation of Edward Denny. He had the money and an interest in the parkland as witness his Pleas of the Forest mentioned earlier in which he sought greater jurisdiction over the commons.

The evidence for this upgrading is contained in the will of James, the second Earl of Carlisle, written in 1660. In this he requests his wife Margaret to have two of the best rooms furnished at Greene Meade Lodge for his godson Edward, this habitation perhaps having attracted the interest of the young Edward whose father, Edward Russell, had purchased Nazeing Bury. We know not whether he ever did inhabit this lodge.

In 1687, as mentioned elsewhere, these properties were dispersed and Thomas Burgh acquired Green Mead and Nazeing Lodge.

The last extant reference to Green Mead seems to be that of Collar writing in 1866 but this may well be apocryphal. Sadly no sign now exists of this hunting lodge but I suggest it stood in the field now known as Green Mead Spring, a large field of some ten acres lying due east of Lodge Farm about half a mile towards the top of the ridge. This has a rather unusual curved shape to its southern corner, bordered by a ditch, perhaps the remains of a moat, from whence an extensive view obtains looking south across the Common towards Waltham Abbey. This would seem an ideal spot for a standing, sited as it is on the high point of Nazeing Common.

John Graham who has farmed these fields for many a year and lives at Lodge Farm has found no signs of any early habitation here but then it would have been a wooden affair of no great durability. I had hoped to find some old timbers incorporated in one of the barns, but a cursory inspection revealed none.

In the New Year of 1997 whilst walking towards this one time scene of the chase we came upon a herd of deer grazing, a magnificent sight, their antlers silhouetted against the sky.

The old cottage on the common by the duck pond which is regarded by some as the site of this standing is undoubtedly 16th.C. but was almost certainly built as a pindar's cottage.[1]

Returning to the subject of the park, a most ambitious piece of construction was undertaken at the same time as the king and his park keeper Sir Anthony Denny was building his new standing, when the whole of Harolds Park, Nazeing Wood and Nazeing Grove were enclosed by fencing. This comprised posts and rails, probably of oak at a total cost, for materials and labour of some £102. This land was then in the possession of the Crown suggesting the Crown footed the bill. This is the first evidence of any large expenditure on the park since its first enclosure nearly four hundred years earlier after it was granted to the abbey by Richard I.

In 1553 this land was gifted by King Edward VI to Joan, Sir Anthony's widow from whom it descended via her son Henry to his son Lord Edward Denny.

Edward Denny was involved in a long argument with the Crown concerning jurisdiction of this parkland. In 1608 he granted it, together with the manor of Nazeing and Harolds Park to James and Honora Hay, the inference being that he had absolute right of disposal. It was then in turn willed to James' son and daughter in law, James and Margaret Hay

In 1651 by an indenture made between himself and the commoners James Hay, the second Earl, conveyed around 475 acres of Nazeing Wood to trustees. This was to be for the use of the tenants of all the ancient houses of Nazeing, there were thought to be 101 of them. In other words, probably under pressure from the aspiring commoners, he made legal the rights which previous lords of the manor had been ignoring.[2]

For his own use he retained two 50 acre portions which were to be attached to 'Nazeing Great Bury and Nazeing Little Bury'[3] together with Green Meade Lodge. This arrangement was subsequently confirmed by the Act of the Protectorate in 1657. Nazeing Wood or Park is born.

The 50 acres to be linked to Nazeing Great Bury probably refers to the strip of land in the North of Nazeing adjoining Broadley Common. He had earlier leased Nazeing Grove just to the West of this.

These various arrangements of James Hay, both concerning the Common and his properties confirm I think that he was residing locally and took an active interest in the affairs of Nazeing.

A draft of the court rolls for 1637 spells out in considerable detail the rules and regulations regarding the common rights. For example only those dwelling in 'ancient tents' (houses) were eligible to common in the wood and there was only to be one commoner per house. Indiscriminate building was frowned upon.

John Payson of Nasinge Berry was debarred from commoning, as were Sir Francis Swift of Nasing Lodge and a Mrs Taylor of Nasinge Vicarage.[3]

These strictures continued as late as 1892 during the tenure of Joseph Pegrum. The presumption of David Pracy and myself is that since these, and later Little Nazeing Bury, were sited on lands of their own, the glebe lands in the case of the vicarage, their tenants were deemed to have a sufficiency of grazing land for their own stock. It is probable that the copyholders, who were well represented at the courts leet, had put their case to this effect towards the end of the previous century when they were particularly active in exerting their rights.

The tenants of Great and Little Nazeingbury were direct tenants of the lords of the manor, they were not copyholders. Nazeing Bury still has no common rights which I have always felt a bit miffed about. Maurice Coleman, one time clerk to the commoners, informed me years ago that one of the Wakes, needing money a while back sold the rights but I think in light of this evidence that was incorrect.

In 1778 William Palmer by an Act of Parliament ensured a more satisfactory management of Nazeing Wood or Park. He was a well-to-do London merchant and subsequently built Nazeing Park. The administration of the Park continues under the trustees as he devised but the function of the park was changed irrevocably following its being ploughed up in 1941 to provide food for the nation and the subsequent 1947 Act authorising its use for farming.

1 ERO T/Z230/19
2 Winters Memorials of the Pilgrim Fathers
3 See chapter 13
4 ERO Winters T/P 140

Celebrating VE-DAY in May 1995

Family croquet at Nazeing Bury in 1996

Chapter 12

The Jones Wake Take Over

Isaac Jones, was a Merchant Taylor based in Broad Street who made, and lost, money by buying and selling mortgages amongst other things. He owned property in Shropshire and Surrey. His son Samuel joined the family business and in 1647 purchased Courteenhall on the outskirts of Northampton, for just under £9000, the domaine that subsequently features large in the history of the Wake family. The Chronological Tree on pages 141-142 renders the following easier to understand.

Isaac was a contemporary of James, the first Earl of Carlisle and of George Lord Goring to whom in 1633 he loaned some £20,000.[1] This considerable sum of money must have been needed by George to pay off some of his debts. Knowing himself to be a beneficiary of his uncle Edward's will he shortly after leased from James, the first Earl of Carlisle, Nazeingbury and other properties which perhaps allayed any unease felt by Isaac as to the soundness of this loan, but he got it wrong; a further forty years passed before it was repaid.

Samuel Jones, resided at Courteenhall whilst continuing to play the property market, journeying to London so to do. He had evidently inherited his father's canny business acumen. At the outset of the Civil War he opted to serve on the Parliamentary side, commanding a regiment of foot and later became an M.P. At the restoration he rather astutely changed sides and raised a loan for the king for which he was rewarded with a knighthood.

He became active in local affairs and was able to indulge his philanthropic nature thanks to his increasing wealth. He built a school at Courteenhall and repaired the church as well as improving other of his estates. In spite of being twice married he died childless, hence he had a succession problem, a recurring fate of the owners of these lands.

In his will dated 1670 [2] he left all his manors and lands to his nephew Samuel Pierrepoint, son of his sister Mary, but owing to the 'idle and unprofitable life' of this gentleman he was dispossessed in a codicil to this will dated 1672, the year of Sir Samuel's death, in favour of the then Samuel Wake. This complicated genealogy is made more explicable by the tree in appendix 1. Sir Samuel Jones had a sister Susan, married to Sir Dru Drury, by whom she had a daughter Diana who in turn married Sir William Wake. This Sir William was the third Baronet, then residing at Piddington in Northamptonshire.

Sir William and Diana, as well as producing the fourth and fifth baronet also sired Samuel, their fifth child; he, Sir Samuel Jones, became heir to his fortune. There were strings attached to this bequest. He was to change his name from Wake to Jones, the estate was to be in the hands of executors until he reached the age of 21 and he was to be educated according 'as my executors and overseer see fit and not as Sir William Wake.' He was also warned to abjure the 'sinns of drunkenesse and debauchery now so much in fashion,' bearing in mind the lately spurned nephew Pierrepoint. We think our current social problems are new!

So Samuel, born in 1670, came into the Wake succession, the lands of Northamptonshire and Essex, litigation having at long last succeeded in wresting the Nazeing estates from the luckless heirs of Lord George Goring.

In this same will Sir Samuel, having commended his soul to God, devised £300 for his tomb to be surmounted by himself and his late wife depicted in a kneeling stance. The result, in Courteenhall church, is a splendidly baroque and sycophantic affair in white marble.To be fair he did leave his new wife well provided for.

Sir Samuel Jones left two astutely chosen executors, Henry Edmonde and Francis Crane, to administer the estates during the minority of his young nephew. They must have spent many hours wading through the relevant documents and their own findings which are on record make convoluted reading:

An indenture of 1679 gives a sobering summary of the vast debts accrued by the Carlisles and the Gorings in their heyday forty years earlier: [2]

Sir William Russell, Margaret Hay's brother, was owed £12,000. This loan was made in 1630, one year before his sister had married the second James.

The Vintner's Company had lost some £24,000.

Robert, Earl of Cork, George Goring's father in law was owed £8,600, borrowed in 1641, which would seem to establish that Lord George Goring was never the absolute owner of the Nazeing estates. The son of the Earl of Cork was finally paid off by Sir Samuel Jones in 1672.

But somehow Sir Samuel's executors, Francis and Crane, managed to pay off these outstanding debts and at the same time acquire the Waltham and Nazing estates which by the end of the 1680's were largely in Wake Jones control. By this time the only living beneficiaries of the original estates, apart possibly from Edward Russell, James' nephew, are the Goring contingent: Charles's widow, Alice and the four ageing sisters, all hoping that some crumbs at least may fall in their direction. Fall it would seem they did since by the end of this decade they had all exchanged their promised property for cash in spite of the afore mentioned encumbrances.

In 1680 Elizabeth Brereton sold her quarter share in Naseingberry, Harolds Park, the Rectory as well as lands meadows and common woods to Jones' executors. Alice followed in 1681 and Diana in 1687.

In 1683 a rival to the Wake Jones dynasty appeared in the

form of Thomas Burgh and his executor Edward Ange who were in the process of acquiring portions from Lady Catherine Scott and Anthony, the son of Mary Deane. This enabled Burgh the possession of Harolds Park, Green Mead, Nazeing Lodge and 50 acres next to Broadley Common - thus initiating further carve up of the one time Denny lands. Incidentally it does seem rather incredible that quarters of the advowson as well as of the vicarage are being dealt out in all apparent seriousness, if the original deeds are to be believed.

Thomas Burgh resided at Harolds Park until his death in 1728, his gravestone is in All Saints church.

Despite that loss, by the time **Samuel Wake Jones** came of age in 1691 he was the proud possessor of a considerable tract of land at Nazeing, including Nazeing Bury and at Waltham Abbey, including the Abbey House in which he took up residence. This was the house built by Edward Denny just 100 years previously.

He entered into the spirit of Essex life, becoming Lord of the Manor of Nazeing, which title has subsequently been handed down the generations of the Wakes to this day. He was also appointed Sheriff of Essex in 1699 and Deputy-Lieutenant in 1711. He married Elizabeth, the daughter of George Champion, an alderman of London, but like his uncle Sir Samuel, sired no heirs, or leastwise no legitimate ones. But he did sire Henry - mother unknown, for at the dawn of the next century, 1709 to be precise, with the strident cry, 'To all Christian People,' Samuel Jones of Waltham Abbey in his will pronounces his son Henry to be the owner of Nazeingbury, but in the same document he then declares that Francis Arundel and Henry Champion, his executors, shall manage the manor of Nasing.[3] Presumably Samuel realised Henry would fade out of the picture having other more spiritual responsibilities as the Bishop of London.

This foreknowledge enabled Samuel, before his death in 1713, to appoint as his putative heir **Charles Wake,** history repeating itself. Charles was his nephew and son of Baldwin Wake, the fifth baronet and Samuel's elder brother. He was perhaps chosen because Samuel realised his succession might enable the continuation of joint holding of the Northampton and Essex estates. In return he was also enjoined to perpetuate the name of Jones. To add to Charles security any surplus rent was to be used for paying off mortgages and buying land in Waltham Abbey and Nazeing.

In 1721 just before Charles Wake attained his majority Henry, 'only son and heir at law' of Samuel Jones did indeed revoke all claims to the Northampton and Essex estates in exchange for £1000.[4]

Born in 1701, Charles was educated at a private boarding school near Enfield and became interested in garden design. In 1724 he moved into the Abbey House, where he mightily improved the garden lay out. He also made changes to the house, the facade of which he had refaced with stone and added entrance pillars, amongst other alterations. Sadly, after his death the house gradually mouldered. In spite of marriage Charles also died childless in 1739. He consequently bequeathed his properties to his nephew Charles, son of his step brother Baldwin Wake.

Charles became the 6th baronet on the death of his grandfather and took the name of **Charles Wake Jones.** He was probably the first Wake to reside at Courteenhall, that manor house acquired by his forbear Sir Samuel Jones, but he also died young in 1755, aged only thirty.

He, being also childless, left his manors in Essex to his cousin William Wake, the eldest son of the 7th baronet . On becoming the 8th in 1765 he remained as straight **Sir William Wake**, there being now no strictures to perpetuate the name of Jones and henceforward the dynastic fortunes of the Wakes remain simpler to understand since direct line inheritance continues until the present day. William married Mary Fenton who, being an heiress, as were conveniently (or probably intentionally) so many of the Wake wives, William was able to build some rather imposing stables at Courteenhall. He spent some time at Waltham, of which he was Lord of the Manor. He was also a member of parliament. After his death in 1785 Lady Wake had all the Waltham papers conveyed to Courteenhall, by which time, if not earlier, the Abbey House was in a state of ruin.

His son, William assumed the title aged seventeen, becoming the ninth baronet. He found another heiress, Mary Sitwell, enabling him to build a new Courteenhall to replace the crumbling old manor house once occupied by Samuel Jones. Mary ensured his succession in the person of Charles, her only child, before she died. Out of the proceeds of her fortune he also purchased some of the tithes at Waltham Abbey. His interests lay largely at the new Courteenhall of which he was very fond in spite of many changes, such as the coming of the railway.

By his second wife, Jenny he produced seven more children and died in 1846, having by then gained the affectionate epithet of '**Old Sir William**.'

At this mid point of the nineteenth century let us take a look at the Nazeing landscape. Land ownership has drastically changed, as related in the Victoria County History. The Wakes have lost and others have gained. Nazeingbury which now represents the remainder of the Wake estates is still listed as the largest holding with 298 acres. The house was tenanted at that time by Edward Collins, farmer.

St. Leonards had 170 acres. This estate had been acquired by James Bury who built and lived in the house of that name, as did his successors after him. Nazeing Lodge comes in at 115 acres and was owned by George Palmer. Lastly, of farms over 100 acres, is Langridge, a farm in the S.W. of Nazeing near to Quenemead. The house of this name is another very old one, having been built around 1540. In addition to these large estates there were many smaller farms.

Old Sir William's son Charles, who inherited this Nazeing Bury portion of Nazeing, was an affable man of indifferent health. After his first wife died he married Charlotte Tait, a delightful lady with a forceful personality whose brother Archie ended up as Archbishop of Canterbury. His influence was often used when family problems got tough. Charles' son William was one of these problems causing considerable concern. In the event he died but a year after his father in 1865. Fortunately he left an heir, Herewald, amongst his several children who succeeded when only seventeen, becoming the twelfth baronet.

Herewald Wake's inheritance was in rather an improvident mess. His estate at Courteenhall comprised 1,629 acres of mixed farm land. Courteenhall itself was in a poor state of repair, which does not say much for its builders after only 100 years, as were several of the farm labourers' cottages. The Essex estate, despite various sales of land, comprised another 1,512 acres. 768 acres of this 'waste within the Manor of Waltham Holy Cross' were sold to the City of London by order of the Epping Forest Commission in 1876. Herewald was much against this plan which he took to adjudication and lost. This has been to the public's gain, contributing towards Epping Forest, a Park for Londoners, and it has remained protected parkland ever since. It now provides the ridge walk from Harolds Park to Waltham Abbey through Ames Green.

Herewald married Catherine St.Aubyn and very gradually they created order, as well as six children.

Because of the cash crisis they had to let Courteenhall for many years, only finally moving back in 1896 when it was thoroughly enjoyed by them and their children. He was a keen farmer and built up a fine stock, in spite of the agricultural depression of the latter part of the 19th century. He also took an active part in local affairs and was patron of the living at Courteenhall church where his brother was installed as curate.

He kept an eye on Waltham and Nazeing activities. Indeed but two weeks before he died in 1916 he had dined with his Waltham Abbey and Nazeing tenants.

He was succeeded by his son **Hereward**, the 13th. baronet. A career soldier who saw action in the Boer War, the Great War, and was also involved in the Second World War. He distinguished himself both on the field and in an administrative capacity. His marriage to Margaret Benson produced seven children including Hereward, the present baronet.

Finances were stretched. The 'Nazeing Estate' was sold in 1919.

Shortly after the last war the government compulsorily purchased a large area of land at Waltham Abbey for housing, the Ninefields Estate. A further area adjacent to the Abbey which had been the Abbey farm and then the abbey gardens was acquired by the Lee Valley Park and has been reinstated into the public gardens.

Finally the 'common land' between Waltham and Nazeing, the site of Waltham Park, Dallance and Holyfields was sold to a gravel extraction company. Thus Sir Hereward, the thirteenth baronet, divested himself of virtually all of the remaining Waltham Estate although his son still holds the title of Lord of the Manor.

He is commemorated by a plaque in All Saints' Church:

To Sir Hereward Wake 13 Baronet 1876-1963.

Vigila et Ora

In 1946 he handed over Courteenhall to his son Hereward who had been spending an eventful time in the army during the war, thereby continuing family tradition.

Hereward was left the rather daunting task, as several of his forbears had been, of yet again pulling the estate together. Initially serious consideration was given to pulling down Courteenhall because of its indifferent state of repair but in the event he had the house and the estate buildings restored. He succeeded as the 14th baronet in 1963.

The Jones and the Wakes between them were Lords of the Manor of Nazeing for some three hundred years and they, or their stewards, during those years presided over the courts, many of which were held at Nazeing Bury, until 1925.

Charles Kingsley's historical romance, '*Hereward the Wake*,' published in 1870, no doubt encouraged the potentiation of the name of Hereward, based as it is on a famous forbear of the present Wake family.

1 HRO D/ELW T84
2 Wake 238
3 Wake 272
4 Wake 366

Nazeing Bury during restoration, 1986, showing English bond

Lodge Farm, Nazeing Common

Chapter 13

Nazeingbury 1600-1950

The next great upgrading of the house, as see chapter 2, occurred at the end of the 17th century. My surmise is that this was executed either by Sir Samuel Jones or his nephew Samuel Wake Jones. We know that before Sir Samuel died in 1672 he had been busy 'improving his estates,' thus implying he had the money so to do. His nephew Samuel twenty years later was left sufficient money, and no doubt encouragement by his indefatigable executors Edmonde and Crane to do likewise. John Walker's suggestion of the date of the facelift in the 1670-80's would seem to support the idea of Sir Samuel having at least incepted the improvements. I continue to favour the idea of the owner having undertaken these works as a capital investment.

During this further extensive renovation, the house was encased in brick, as shown in the photo on the opposite page, leaving the structural timbers in situ although the middle was projected forward and the front door moved to its present central position. Brickwork laid in English bond above this door is shown in the photograph taken during repair work. This no doubt involved fairly extensive internal remodelling, including the raising of the roof.

John Walker has described the further face lift in 1765 during the ownership of William Wake the 8th baronet, he who built the stable block at Courteenhall.

The next large building project took place in the early 1800's as already described. This addition comprised a wing north of and coterminous with the previous structure thereby doubling the size of the house. The rear elevation remains unfaced and is of red brick also in English bond although not so finely pointed as is the older building. A further chimney was built to service the kitchen range. At some stage a chimney had been added on the eastern end of the older building thus allowing heating to that end of the house. When removing one of these fireplaces we came upon a vast number of oyster shells in the cavity behind.

This extension provided on the ground floor a large room subsequently used as a billiard room and a room adjacent occupying two floors with a staircase and balcony giving access to the first floor. This served as a kitchen and had a hatchway through to the dining room. Upstairs three further bedrooms were created connected by a separate corridor.

A Mr William Welch 'gentleman,' leased the house for several years from 1795 and may have been responsible for this extension. Sir Herewald Wake, the 12th baronet was the landlord and, as we have seen, an enthusiastic landowner but limited for funds. But, whoever was responsible, one of the purposes may have been to provide extra accommodation for farm workers. As detailed later Joseph Pegrum accommodated farm labourers, rather against his will, which same necessity may well have obtained at the beginning of the century.

Some time around mid century a single storey extension was thrown out behind this wing to serve as a dairy, which has now been upgraded to a surgery.

We have found disappointingly few artefacts during our years of residence apart from those mentioned above, this in spite of fairly diligent searching by ourselves and our children. A sweep in the garden with a metal detector merely uncovered an early 20th century silver bracelet and several horseshoes.

So during these three hundred years whilst its appearance has changed its prime function has remained as a dwelling place for the succession of farmers and their families who have been 'tilling the soil.' It has also continued to host the Manor Courts.

I have mentioned John (Pason) Payson, a known resident at the Berri in 1637. He was married to Lydia, who died in 1647 and had two children, John born in 1637 and Joseph who died in infancy in 1645. In 1640 he was serving as a church warden. His name is the earliest listed as being debarred from commoning and in that same year of 1637 he was one of several threatened with a five shilling fine if he failed to 'make his fence against the marsh'.

In 1643 his name is one of thirty odd in Nazing whose land was sequestered, suggesting he was of royalist persuasion, which is very likely since he was a tenant of the younger James, Earl of Carlisle whose land was also sequestered, being a 'delinquent'.

For the Manor of Nazing a list is preserved of its tenant farmers and their annual rents for the year 1660,[1] the total income being over one thousand pounds. Included in these twenty-six names, several of whom crop up in the parish register, is that of John Payson, probably the same whose land had earlier been sequestered and still residing at Nazeing Bury.

The leaseholder in 1672 was William Foord, who earlier suffered litigation concerning his lease. He must have won since he was still the tenant in 1690 when Lydia Foord, 'daughter of William Foord of Nazing Berry' was baptised.[2]

In 1709 Nazeingbury was in the occupation of Randolph Lawrence and his undertenants where he probably remained until shortly before his death in 1741. He also is specifically abjured from commoning. His yearly rent in 1709 was £134 whilst Little Nazeingbury at that time was rented for £85.

John Lake and his wife Ann became tenants in 1740, shortly before Randolph Lawrence died, he having acquired other copyhold premises for his wife. A later document recording the lease between Sir William Wake and John Lake adds the rider that it is up to Lake to keep up the public roads, the gravel being taken from the local pits - just an example of the multifarious responsibilities of tenancy in those days. The gravel industry, which still continues, was evidently already operating even then.

The Lake tenancy ceased in 1784 by which time the rent had been increased to £184-15 and they were followed by James Goodwin who remained until 1796. According to a valuation made at that time Mr Goodwin is said to have 'farmed it fairly and kept up the repairs and the fences although he does not appear to have made much improvement, nor do I think it likely he will.' The valuer continues: 'If this farm was let, some person from town would be likely to have it at a good price; for the conveniency of having so good a house and garden and would not take less than £320 p.a.'2

Throughout the 17th and18th centuries references have been made to a **Nazeing Great Bury** and a **Nazeing Little Bury.** Nazeing Great Bury and Nazeingbury are one and the same, being also sometimes referred to simply as the Berri or the Manor House. But there was also in existence between roughly 1650 and 1860 a 'Nazeing Little Bury', location unknown. Common land assigned to it, another fifty acres, was next to Green Mead. It is recorded as being tenanted by Thomas Watts at a yearly rental of fourscore and five pounds. This in 1709. At the end of the same century by a Thomas Want for £175-10, implying a substantial property since this rental was not much less than that for the Bury itself. Collar mentions it in his 1866 work as being in the ownership of George Palmer, the then owner of Nazeing Park, although this could have been hearsay. So far as we are aware no trace now remains. David Pracy and I suspect it may have been by the river near where The Crown public house is now and where the toll bridge was.

Following the death of William the 8th baronet in 1785

his son, another William, in 1792 embarked on the building of a new Courteenhall, aided by his wife's hefty dowry of £25,000. He leased the manors of Waltham and Nazeingbury, together with the rectory, to Petre and John Leathers which lease three years later was acquired by William Welch, a name that continues to this day in Nazeing history, for a further 15 years.[3] But James Goodwin whose presence in 1784 is attested by the court rolls continued in residence at least until the valuation in 1796. A marginal note in the court record for 1785 has a reminder for the steward to leave a copy 'at Mr. James Goodwin at the Manor House.'

Probably William Welch 'gentleman' moved in then for a few years, he who possibly built the rear wing.

At Michaelmas 1812 Sir William Wake leased Nazeing Great Bury Farm to **William Collins.**[4] He and his wife Mary had lived at Moulton, Northants for some while, probably as tenants of Sir William. Their son Edward had been baptised at Moulton Parish church in 1797. A twelve year lease was agreed, to expire in 1824. I reproduce part of the text of this lease, with some added punctuation, since the names seem so evocative of times gone by:

> "And those pieces or parcels of arable land called Great West Field, Great Black Lands, Middle Black Lands, Further Black Lands, the Thorlands in eight several fields, Half Field, Three Acres, Five Acres , Trats Field , Claytons, Amberlands, Four Acres , Little West Field, and a spinney called Cobbfield. Containing in the whole by assesment one hundred and seventy three acres one rood and four perches be the same more or less. And also several Fields or closes, pieces or parcels of meadows or pasture land called the Great Hoppitt , the Little Hoppitt, the five acres, Little Westfield, Natbocks Mead, Great Hawmead, Little Hawmead, Great Quene mead, Little Queen Mead, Sum-

mer Lease, the Holme Gravel Pitt Field , and Great Westfield; containing together by assessment one hundred and twenty three acres. And all those twelve acres of Meadow be the same more or less in a certain country mead called Nazeing Mead. And also those forty cow leezes or pasturage for forty cows in a certain Common Marsh called Nazeing Marsh. And also that pasture field commonly called Upper West Field containing by estimation four acres and two acres more or less of the Common Field called Stone Shot, a horse grass in Nazeing Marsh.

And also that piece or parcel of land lately enclosed from the waste and now and for some time past used as an orchard to the said capital messuage containing by estimation half an acre be the same more or less. And those two fields, Little Langfords otherwise Little Langfield and Bean field."

The holding of the Courts Leet must be held there when and as necessary.

A few of these names still exist as for example Langfields, a field of some seventeen acres now occupied by the houses of Highland road and Shooters Drive. The map commissioned by Sir William Wake, 1767, (pp58-59) depicts most of these named fields, the tithe map of 1847 likewise. A project is currently afoot [1997], the Essex Place-names Project, to ascertain whether these fields still survive and if so in what state they are now. We will no doubt find many changes have occurred during these last one hundred years.

A very comprehensive parish survey was undertaken of the lands of Nazeing in 1824. The resulting copperplate script lists all the owners, the tenants of their lands, and the rental. The map produced at the same time shows these properties in detail. The Wake possessions, now occupying perhaps a third of the total.

The Collins were evidently satisfactory tenants, an added bonus no doubt being their acquaintenceship with Sir William. But when William Collins died in 1838 a fresh indenture had to be drawn up between Sir William and Mary and Edward Collins her son.

But it transpired that William had been a bit neglectful of repairs on the house and the outbuildings, his widow Mary being obliged, at her own expense, to have these put into good and tenantable repair.[3] That same condition of tenants being responsible for repairs as had applied in the year 1502 when John Nankotton took up the lease.

The 1841 census return for Nazeing shows Edward Collins as head of the household, with his mother still resident, farming 300 acres. He was evidently a bachelor since in 1851, Mary having died, she is replaced by Esther Lewis the housekeeper.

In 1854 Edward took on additional duties as gamekeeper, confirming his continuing esteem in the eyes of the Wake family, 'Old Sir William' having by now been succeeded by his son Charles. Around this time Sir Charles authorised and presumably paid for the construction of a rather elaborate brick and wooden building for housing chickens.[5] By the time of the next census in 1861 Edward's household had been enlarged to include, as well as Esther his faithful housekeeper, Elizabeth the dairymaid, hence his need of the dairy together with Thomas a servant. Ten years later, at the age of seventy four, his establishment remained basically the same.

Sometime in the late 1870's the long tenure of the Collins family came to an end. In their stead arrived Joseph and Susannah **Pegrum**. Pegrums, or Pigrams, have flourished in Nazeing for many generations, featuring prominently in the parish register since its inception and subsequently the Congregational register as they were later stalwarts of that church.

Joseph Pegrum married Susannah, Suey, his cousin. Joseph's family lived at Greenleaves, a house mentioned by John Walker, in Hoe Lane which has recently been carefully restored by Daphne and Ed Borton and is most attractive in its garden setting.

Suey, another Pegrum, lived during childhood at Ninnings in Middle Street, where her parents had moved soon after their marriage; another attractive and well looked after old house.

Joseph and Suey both of whom were born in 1847 had moved to the Bury as leaseholders by at least 1881 where they lived and farmed for just on forty years. Joseph was a man of some importance in the village, being a deacon of his chapel, a trustee of the Common, in spite of having no common rights, and an elected member of the Epping Rural District Council. In the year of 1881 they employed as servants Henry Starling and Alice Pegrum. Ten years later their family comprised Edith, Agnes, Hilda and David, together with two fifteen year old servant girls.

For the photograph of their golden jubilee in 1897 depicting themselves and some sixty members of their extended family outside the house; see page 52. At that time the Pegrums and their relations between them occupied several of the old houses of Nazeing including Darmers, Camps and Smalldrinks.

In 1919 Joseph, having been a tenant for some forty years, was able to purchase at auction the Nazeing Estate, comprising the house and farmland from Sir Hereward for £10,000. Thus owner and tenant became one for the first time in its history.

A sale catalogue of Savill's dated 1919 gives a useful description of the property at Nazeing Bury at this time:

Ground floor: Lounge hall, drawing room, dining room, kitchen, larder, dairy, scullery and cellar.

Above: 6 bedrooms. 2 attic rooms.

Outbuildings: wood and coal sheds, cooling house, well house with tank.

Farm buildings were brick and tiled ranged round three yards and included stabling, cow houses and a poultry house, [that authorised by Sir Charles Wake].

In addition was listed a kitchen garden and an orchard which extended east from the house as far as North Street. Included were other parcels of land to the north and south of the house, 266 acres in all.[6]

Dallance, another property of Sir Hereward's and the one time home of the Dennys', also features in this same catalogue.

The disposition of the internal rooms is much as it is now, of the outbuildings only the well house survives, but minus its tank. A delightful old man, a former patient of mine, Bogey Hutchings, once recalled to me his time as a shepherd on the farm as a young man and remembered a horse walking round this structure drawing up water from the well, said to be some 90 feet deep. This well probably still exists under the concrete floor which I have hesitated to disturb but am tempted!

David, Joseph's son, commenced his working life farming at the old family home of Greenleaves, but not being taken by this manner of life in 1922 his father loaned him some £3000 to build the Langfield Estate on the fields aforementioned. These were houses built on Nazeing Bury land sold to Joseph by Hereward Wake. Structurally they were very good, as witness their present existence, but financially unsound, having cost more to build than to sell, the depression at that time not helping any.

Joseph only lived in the house as owner for a short while. In the same year his son set up as a builder, he and his wife Suey moved to Newlands, a smaller property in Middle Street, selling Nazeing Bury and the farm to Walter Benjafield for £11,000, so he still made a profit.

His stock was auctioned separately and included 23 horses, 49 cows and heifers, 3 bulls and 225 sheep as well as much other farm impedimenta. He must have been sad to see it go but being by then aged 75 and his son David having opted out of farming he had no option. He died in 1936.

Farming

We tend to regard farming of yore as having been a rather idyllic pastime but this was by no means invariably so. When Joseph was farming he was enduring the financial depression of that time exacerbated by exceptionally poor weather conditions and cheap continental imports - a recurring cry.[7] Farms were labour intensive, Joseph was employing almost forty hands, which added considerably to the costs and landlords did what they could to maintain viability such as reducing rents and provide accommodation.

In 1901 Rider Haggard, more commonly associated with *King Solomon's Mines,* conducted a large survey of the English agricultural scene and he recalls a meeting he had with Joseph Pegrum.[8] At that time Joseph was actually farming 600 acres. 'Things could not look worse. A farmer had to live like a labourer, they were wasting rather than strengthening.' Skilled labour was hard to find. The district, he said was badly off for cottages so he had to take bachelors in to board. In a neighbouring farm Haggard records being shown a small windowless barn in which twenty men slept upon the floor. This brings to my mind the immigrant Sicilian labour brought in to man the glass house industry hereabouts in the 1950's, local labour having priced itself out of the market. They also dossed down in crowded sheds in most unsalubrious conditions.

Mr Pegrum concluded by mentioning his various sources of income - milk, hay, sheep and sometimes potatoes although this could be a difficult crop to market. In view of this state of affairs it is hardly surprising that son David took to an alternative occupation.

Following the long incumbency of Joseph and Suey ownership of Nazeing Bury becomes indisputable since abstracts and title deeds are in my possession. These actually make very dull reading, the first being dated 1955. Another cache of papers has given us further information regarding property prices and so forth.9

In addition the recollections of the living now help to enliven the scene. Ethel, **Walter Benjafield**'s daughter, when she revisited the house in 1992 gave us some anecdotes, as did Harold, his son and his wife more recently. Her father was involved in mixed farming, cattle and sheep on the still extant 266 acres. He owned no tractor, ploughing being carried out by horse drawn machinery.

He traded livestock by playing the markets and would for example buy cows in calf from Chelmsford and sell the calves as far away as Salisbury if the prices were right. The animals would be walked to Broxbourne station and entrained.

The orchard was thriving then and apples were stored in the attic and a tennis court adorned the front garden. There being by now mains water, her father installed a bathroom and internal toilet on the first floor, dividing a larger bedroom on the S.E. of the house. He also had mains electricity connected.

Harold recalled being banished to the attic when suffering from scarlet fever but has otherwise fond memories of the house.

In the twenties the financial return was declining on dairy farming thus Walter Benjafield was one of the first to commence the Lea Valley glass house industry, selling off his fields to finance this. He built glass houses along what is now Nursery Road, on his own farm land, which industry his son Harold continued.

The Carthagena estate was developed for those wanting weekend retreats from London. Houses were built to accommodate the nursery workers and more land was sold for other developments. Hence in the short space of eight years Nazeing Bury itself was converted from a farm to a private residence. The urban sprawl was gaining pace.

In 1929 Walter Benjafield moved to Bury Close, Nazeing, continuing his nursery business. He sold Nazeing Bury, together with just two acres which included the orchard, to Reginald Christie for £2,800, retaining several acres which he gradually sold off during the following years.

Mr. and Mrs **Reginald Christie** were resident from 1929 until 1942. He was a retired Scots engineer, whilst she was an imposing lady who already had two children from her first marriage. Soon after we had moved in my wife met a former knowledgeable Nazeing resident Cinderella Sainsbury who had been a friend of Mrs Christie. She described her as having had extremely good style in interior design with 'a wonderful taste in lamp shades my dear.' Another visitor, who came with a photograph of himself aged ten climbing the pine tree, recalled that the Christie's employed a butler, would dress for dinner and that there was a billiard room in the long back room. Thus it was probably Mr Christie who panelled this room, if only in dark stained plywood, as well as redecorating the rest of the house.

Surrounding the house then was just over two acres of garden, including the orchard, together with some outbuildings, all I have no doubt in very good order until the onset of the war.

In 1942 the house was sold for £3250 to the **United Flexible Metallic Tubing Co**. So from an era 'where all's accustomed, ceremonious,' [Yeats,] to one of practical necessity. The company, who made aircraft engines, needed a subsidiary factory in case they got bombed out from their working factory. A substantial ugly brick building was therefore constructed north of the house. The house remained tenanted and even had a new electricity system installed. During this tenancy a small parcel of land at the N.W. corner of the adjacent crossroads was sold to the highways department. Whether any engines were made in this building I know not but after the war the company continued to justify their name by manufacturing metal tubes, both the director and some of the employees inhabiting the house. 10

In 1955 this company departed, having first enriched themselves by selling off the orchard which had existed for at least a hundred and fifty years. A chain link fence was erected on the new boundary and houses built down North Street and round the corner into Nazeing Road where apple trees used to flourish. In fact a few remained in the gardens of these houses until quite recently. The house and about an acre of remaining land was bought by **Frederick Cayford** for £4000.

For five years the Cayford brothers and their families used the one time factory building for mushroom growing, they also built a glass house on its northern side.

Most of the other properties mentioned in this treatise are still extant:

Harolds Park which has featured quite large is a very active farm. The house itself has been largely rebuilt. Amongst other vicissitudes it was early inhabited by Sir Edward Greville. He married Elizabeth Grey after the death of her first husband

Henry Denny, Sir Anthony Denny's son. It then went to Sir Francis Swift, Greville's son in law and later to Thomas Burgh. From 1954 it was the residence of Lord John Mackie of Bumbles Green who lived and farmed there whilst following his parliamentary, forestry and many other activities, local and national. He has now been succeeded by his son George and family.

Nazeing Lodge, now as I have mentioned known as Lodge farm, is thriving, John Graham and his son Robert farming the fields of Nazeing Common, Green Mead and thereabouts.

Langridge Farm is rather exceptional amongst these houses of Nazeing in that it has been a freehold since medieval times and has continued in private hands until the present day, although its surrounding acres have been exploited for gravel, leaving the house on an island. Happily the land is now being reinstated.

Claverhambury, secluded near Ames Green, is home to greyhounds.

Sewardstonebury south of Waltham Abbey is rather encroached upon by more recent building.

Courteenhall, home of the Wakes for so many years is still very much in existence. In the summer of 1996 Sir Hereward kindly invited Margaret and myself for a visit.

Sir Hereward is still The Lord of The Manor of Nazeing, although as he acknowledged, somewhat wistfully I thought, the title is merely titular: he holding now no estate in Nazeing.

The buildings at Courteenhall are all of the local golden limestone. The oldest is the medieval church, a structure of charm forming a repository for Wake forbears. The earliest of these is Richard Ouseley who married Magdalen Wake and built the original manor house subsequently purchased by Samuel Jones. His monument is a large slab of black purbeck marble dated 1599.

Both Samuel Jones' are buried here, the former with aforementioned elaborate white Italian marble effigy . This has been recently cleaned under the instructions of Sir Hereward who has spent a commendable amount of time and money in preserving these monuments and buildings. Most of the Wake ancestors are also remembered here or in the churchyard.

Looking North from the church the parkland slopes away towards a view of the 'new' Courteenhall sited attractively between Sir Hereward's arboretum on the right and the stable block, now converted to residences, on the left.

Courteenhall itself, which was lovingly restored in 1953 by Sir Hereward, is now inhabited by his son, he and Lady Julia having recently moved, following further restoration work, to the Old School House. This is that very same school built by the order of the first Sir Samuel Jones for the free teaching of local boys in 1672. It continued as a school until the end of the last century. The school room itself is now restored and preserved for local functions. A large rectangular room, it contains around its periphery the original wooden desks and benches for its young pupils with their initials still carved thereon.

1 Wake 232 2 Wake X2747

3 Wake box X2737 4 ibid.

5 Wake box on shelf 6 ERO 19/9

7 G.E,Mingay *The Gentry* 1976

8 Rider Haggard *Rural England*

9 From documents sorted by David Pracy in the possession of Mr & Mrs John Goulding

10 Recollections of Mrs. Marion Whittaker. She and her husband had a bedsit in the very room I have been writing this.

The Gervis Family
at Nazeing Bury for a Party
April 1996

Chapter 14

Gervis Arrival ~ 1960

I have explained earlier how we acquired the house. The previous owners had rather concentrated on growing mushrooms at the expense of home maintenance and this showed.

The surveyor's conclusion was of multiple defects from top to bottom or roof tiles to the drains. We decided that since it had evidently weathered some 400 years it would likely continue upright for our lifetime and purchased it for £5000, which seemed a lot of money then but an inconsiderable sum nowadays!

Fortunately we have been proved correct so far. A good structure, like a living organism, whether animal or vegetable, should be capable of surviving and evolving and this ability Nazeing Bury has most eminently demonstrated.

Moving from a small boat and transient homes we found this large house rather empty. Fortunately at that time there took place most Thursdays, my half day, excellent auctions of furniture, carpets, bedding and all sorts, so furnishing gradually took place. We now seem to provide storage space for our children's possessions for which they have no room.

We were constrained to renovate the roof which was pervious in places to rain and snow. Remarkably, only two timbers needed replacing, a testament to the durability of oak. During the reroofing we also took the opportunity to install two attic skylights, having first removed a low false ceiling, thereby revealing a lot more of the superb old oaken beams.

Painting and decorating is a fairly continuous process and to facilitate it I still use the one time billiard room as a very satisfactory workshop. A downstairs cloakroom and a second upstairs bathroom were ingeniously devised by my architect brother out of the space of the old back kitchen, but still leaving a sufficient playroom for the children.

Externally the paint and plaster fell off fairly regularly in the winter frosts, a process mercifully halted by the insertion of an injected damp course in 1985.The following summer we undertook a major external renovation of this facing, with the invaluable help of Alf Hilling, a congenial and knowledgeable local man. We removed all loose stucco, thereby revealing the old red bricks and soundly renewed same with a lime mortar where it has remained ever since.

The garden to the South of the house extends to the roadway near where is an old Chile pine. A beech hedge, planted in 1989, marks the eastern boundary and on the other side is the old brick wall now topped by fencing. This was punctuated near the house by a gateway which would have led into the farm yard and the former barns. Supposedly, a knight in full armour would on occasions be seen but, contrary to popular belief, we have never encountered a ghost.

For a while we had a tennis court, little realising we were following thereby the Benjafield tradition of fifty years earlier. This same grassy sward has served for many purposes ranging from local bazaars to croquet. The avenue of Acer Cappadocicum Rubrum was planted in 1986 and a composite brick driveway replaced the old potted gravel track a few years later.

Since our earliest days here we have enjoyed growing vegetables, with varying degrees of success. At one stage the weeds were winning until our daughter Rachael came to my rescue. Latterly success has been greater, stimulated by the hope of a prize at the Nazeing Horticultural shows; in any event it is gratifying to grow and eat our own produce.

Adaptable as it has proved materially, so has Nazeing Bury been in a social context. Increasing family, family and friendly gatherings, indoor and outdoor occasions, it has harboured them all, as Margaret shortly elaborates.

Chapter 15

General Practice

Dr. David Knight in his book, 'Then Now and Then What,' gives an interesting account of Hoddesdon and its doctors during the past two centuries, with particular reference to his own former practice. When I arrived in 1959 there were four practices in Hoddesdon, each at that time of three partners. By a tacit understanding Nazeing was to a great extent shared between Dr. Dimock's Broxbourne practice and our own. Both practices considered a branch surgery in Nazeing would be welcomed by the local residents, in particular mothers with young children, public transport being a trifle infrequent and not every family having their own car.

As Dr Dimock's new boy, Dr. Sutherland had already been set up with a branch surgery beside the newly erected shops at Langley Green. The practice I joined had its main surgery at 56 The High Street, Hoddesdon, a most attractive Queen Anne building. As I mentioned in my introduction, a house - one of several barely completed in Middle Street adjoining The Crooked Billet - had been purchased and in this we lived for a year, the dining room doubling up as a consulting room and a small extension at the back as a waiting room. With three young children and a dog and the 'garden' a sea of mud, life, especially for Margaret, at times lacked tranquillity. The expansion into Nazeing Bury was a relief to everyone.

The old dairy at the back of the house was converted into a small but satisfactory surgery and waiting room. This had the great advantage of separation from the house and direct access for the patients. Between us we held a daily surgery, a routine continued to this day by my former partners. I think most patients shared my personal appreciation of the informal set up, no appointment system but facilities for a consultation, some simple diagnostic procedures and the issuing of prescriptions as necessary.

By this time Dr. Sutherland and his partners had moved their branch to premises above the chemist's shop on Nazeingbury Parade where they also continue to consult.

Between them these two practices now largely look after the Nazeing residents. We used to have a foot in Roydon, Leslie Roe and I each doing a weekly surgery in the Roydon Village Hall, a rather primitive procedure long discontinued.

In the 60's general practice was perhaps more personal than nowadays, partly due to fewer doctors and patients. Form filling and administration played a minor role, all in the capable hands of the aforementioned Ann Cayford. Living as it were 'above the shop' at Nazeing Bury resulted in a feeling of togetherness with my patients, although there were times when I wished them further away! Margaret's feedback, gleaned while shopping on the parade also proved interesting. Home visiting was greater, partly due to lack of transport and also perhaps to a higher rate of repeat visits to house bound patients.

Each practice ran its own on-call system which initially meant a rota of one in three; this could prove a rather exhausting burden, although since we were acquainted with most of the patients who rang we were often able to administer advice by phone. In those days most babies were delivered at home, I am sure a more satisfying process for the mothers.

Over the following years all the partnerships increased in size and grew out of their premises. We, with some reservations, moved into the newly constructed Health Centre situated on the High Street next to Lowewood, the old library. This gave us proximity to our health visitors and other facilities but by the time there were six of us we were well and truly cramped and remained so in spite of many pleas to the powers that were supposed to solve those matters. Finally in desperation we moved into The Limes in Conduit Lane, a newly constructed office block where the practice has remained more or less satisfactorily ever since.

By about 1965 several younger doctors were practising in the immediate area so we set up a 'young doctors group.' Bobby Sutherland, having by then acquired his own house, hosted us there of an evening on an approximately monthly basis and aided by a little beer, we discussed matters of medical interest. A few years later the venue was changed to Nazeing Bury and continued there until my retirement. These occasions proved a pleasant means of meeting our colleagues and local consultants who kindly agreed to talk to us. On two occasions we organised parties to which we invited some of our hospital consultants together with their wives which further fostered friendships. This society, still extant, is now known as the Sutherland Society in memory of Bobby.

Margaret, 1985

Chapter 16

The Spirit of the House, by Margaret

I have found it difficult to know where to begin in writing about the house. I move from room to room, each with its own atmosphere and memories. I therefore return to the heart of the house, the kitchen, as it is here that I am most at home.

It is January 1997 and very cold outside, but inside it is warm with the aroma of the soup bubbling on the Esse. It is a loved home.

However our first winter in Nazeing Bury was a very different story. John has already described how we acquired Nazeing Bury but not our parents' reaction. It was unfortunate that the weather was dour on the days they visited and their reactions were similar - dismay if not horror; nevertheless they helped enormously. My mother-in-law would often make suggestions as to ways of tackling problems in the house or garden. She was nearly always right and many of her ideas we implemented with great success.

We had moved in on June 1st 1960, a rather wet day. The children, Caroline aged four, Rachael aged three and Mark, mobile aged fourteen months, quickly learned that they could be out of sight and ear-shot, at times becoming totally lost, which I think worried me more than them.

The installation of the Esse stove began the creation of the heart of the house. It started life as a solid fuel burner, later being converted to oil, it is now fired by gas and still going strong. So this room became the kitchen and remains so today, despite various changes over the years.

Another priority was to establish the surgery, which did not come without its problems. One of these was keeping the children quiet and away from the surgery whilst it was in progress, because some of them did rather enjoy socialising. Another problem was sound-proofing. In my larder I could hear what was said, not in the consulting room but in the waiting-room, between patients waiting to see the doctor. One day I heard one patient say to another: "Have you met the new doctor?" The reply was "Yes, he is very nice, but his wife is a real old dragon." I never listened again. Occasionally we have found patients waiting in the hall in the mistaken belief they were in the surgery waiting room!

Over the years I have enjoyed contact with the patients and this stimulated my interest in community affairs such as the mother and baby clinic. Later I was asked by the Conservatives to be their candidate for the Nazeingbury ward of the parish council but I came to feel that this should not be a political platform so next time I stood as an Independent. I felt much more comfortable with this label but some of my fellow councillors had their doubts! My work on this council led to the formation, jointly with Denis Driver another councillor, of the Association for the Elderly and the Handicapped, now in its twenty-sixth year.

Our fourth child, Nigel, was born three months after we moved in, thus rounding up our family nicely to two girls and two boys, or so we thought. Needing help badly we were extemely lucky to enlist Phil McAleer, a wonderful person who could turn her hand to anything, from amusing the children to gardening and decorating. Those first few years I could not have managed without her, she helped me from 2 - 6 pm on weekdays and later would take charge of the children if we were away. The children were a little in awe of her much needed discipline but nevertheless still love her dearly. She has now moved to Northamptonshire but we still keep in touch.

Entry to the house is through the front door into **The Hall**. This is a delightful large, beamed room, probably the oldest room in the house.It is the principal reception room where everything happened, including the holding of the courts and other social events of the village. Floored with very old flag stones it has a large inglenook fireplace taking up most of one wall and furnished with a wooden doored proving oven on one side and a recess for salt on the other. There are wooden pews on either side of the fireplace, we do not know when these were installed.

The room comes into its own when there is a party, especially at Christmas. In our early years we put up an enormous curtain suspended from the main beam, to cut out some of the draughts and concentrate the warmth. When we were more than just family we would sometimes eat out there, the light of the fire and candles creating a romantic atmosphere. The children also used the curtain when performing their little dramas. We still have dramatic presentations in this hall, performed by grandchildren and their friends, but now entrances and exits are from the stairway, as on the staircase there is a large door with a viewing flap so actors can time their entrances to best effect.

We needed to paint the hall because when we moved in the room had been used just as a passageway and was a drab cream completely lacking life. Having redecorated we were left with an ugly box by the front door which housed old electrics. John enquired of the electricity board whether he could safely disconnect and was given the go-ahead. Having removed the box he proceeded to cut the cable when there was a mighty flash and bang and we were plunged into darkness. John, who fortunately was wearing rubber boots, was flung across the room with a wooden handle of the melted saw in his hands. Not only had our electricity blown but the street lights were also out. The electricity board agreed the cable was not dead! They came and cordoned off the surrounding area and subsequently disconnected and made good. No sign now remains of this drama, but perhaps we should put up a plaque?

The Playroom. Behind the heart of the house, our present kitchen, is a strange high room. In times past this was the kitchen used by servants, food being prepared there and then served through a hatchway to the dining room, now our kitchen.When we arrived it was still used for cooking, there being a large earthenware sink and an alcove where once the oven had been. Ranged around the entire room were myriad pipes and high up on one wall two tiers of primitive, but functioning, fuse boxes installed during the war when the house had been used for offices. It was an extremely antiquated system and one of the priorities of our house survey in 1959 was to rewire the house; this we eventually did in 1987. Until then we were dogged by blowing fuses, especially in the early days, and that always seemed to happen just as we put all the little dears in the bath. Torches and candles were always at the ready, together with a step ladder to reach the boxes and replace the offending fuse. Satisfaction was tempered with despair as one viewed the ravages of the water fight that had meanwhile ensued by candlelight.

We made this room into a utility and children's play area in which we installed a large trampoline. This was enjoyed by the children as well as by a pet goat who would enter from the garden, jump on to the trampoline and then through the hatchway into the kitchen with an eye to any titbits. The washing machine was also kept in here and besides its obvious use, the children found this a useful repository. One day when I had kittens ready to go to a new home, the new owners arrived and search as we did we could not find the kittens. Several hours later when I went to do some washing two little faces peered out at me from the round window, they nearly had a watery grave. I knew the children did not want them to go to their new home, so they had hidden them!

To paint the playroom we must have employed the smallest man in the south of England. Unfortunately he did not like heights which did not help in decorating such a high room, but with John's help he managed. He used to spend some lunch times in the hall fireplace since he had been told that King Harold had signed the beam with K H, but sadly he never found it!

This room remained the same until about 1975 when we closed the hatch, turned the stairs around and put in a cloakroom below and another bathroom above. Later still when the trampoline was long gone John put in a false ceiling which helped to make this a more comfortable room which is still used as a play area by the grandchildren and a television room for all.

Workroom Adjoining was a room extending along the back of the house which John used as a workshop; he later allowed me a small area of this as a dining room. It was from this workshop that the central heating system was created at long last in 1964.

A great friend of ours who knew about such things suggested a hot air system so the room became filled with many sheets of metal, the potential ducts. Nothing daunted John gradually extended this ducting throughout the house. All this he did in his off duty hours over the course of a year or so.

The great day came when the biggest and oldest reconditioned boiler arrived and with some difficulty was manouvred into the workroom. Having been connected by professionals it roared into life and worked like a dream albeit rather a noisy one. After twenty years this boiler was replaced by a gas fired one, quieter and more efficient but not so exciting.

The Study. The next room to be tackled was the reception room to the left of the front door. This had an ugly modern little hearth, extremely damp walls and bindweed growing up through the floor boards, around and inside the windows and into the shutters, which however attractive was not very practical for a living room. One day when I was out with the children John decided to surprise me. When he opened the door to us on our return the original fireplace had been uncovered and everything, including John, was covered in soot.

Having removed an inbuilt brick chimney we were left with another inglenook fireplace, mirror to the one in the hall. After some experimentation and the fitting of a hood we ended up with a very pleasing fireplace backed by original Tudor herringbone brickwork.

This room has south and west facing windows, which as with the other south facing rooms all have the original wooden shutters, still used on occasions. The west facing window we subsequently replaced by a more convenient doorway leading to the adjacent side garden. We are fortunate to have original early 19th century brass door furniture.

Having overcome the fundamental problems we decorated this as my dream elegant 'withdrawing room.' The paintwork was in white and I chose a sedate Edwardian grey and white striped paper. We decided to light a fire and sit and contemplate the room and saw that it was good.

Unfortunately during the night a log fell out of the firebasket onto another log which smouldered but did not catch fire. The next morning I felt the heat as I approached the room and when I opened the door the room was completely smoke and soot covered and festooned with amazing grey cobweb like strands. It looked as if it had been shut up for a hundred years. Back to square one. We abandoned the grand for the practical, we cleaned down the paintwork and emulsioned the walls. Goodbye to a dream room.

The Flat. Another task was to create a flat out of two surplus bedrooms to help defray expenses, the two rooms on the western side of the house, one of which had been set aside for old Mrs. Ramsey and her feather bed in 1569. This flat was initially made for Bobby Sutherland who had arrived in Nazeing a few months before us. At that time he was a bachelor and living in rented accommodation and seemed grateful for this offer even though conditions were somewhat primitive and he had to share the one and only bathroom. This worked extremely well until he bought his own house.

We have continued to provide a flat in the house which by and large has proved satisfactory, especially after the addition of a second bathroom.

These were happy times and the children loved it when Bobby appeared, as he often did, at tea time. After a few minutes of being bombarded physically and noisily he would usually remember he had an urgent visit to make and disappeared quickly! He sometimes had his brother to stay, another doctor at that time in the Navy. They made a splendid duo, especially at Christmas time, when they would help John and me fill the childrens' stockings, amidst great hilarity.

The patients at times found it a bit confusing, two doctors under one roof, but from different practices; they were somehow expected to be rivals - which of course they were not - rather having much in common beside their work and we all remained firm friends until he died in 1992, an occasion of great sadness to many. Bobby and John together planted a blue cedar in the front garden, now quite a majestic tree.

Attic Rooms Other bedrooms were made more habitable for children and visitors over a period of time. The attic rooms were extremely cold and basic so when we eventually succumbed to television that is where it went. We needed to want to watch a programme very badly and had to put on layers of clothing, as if going to the North Pole. This was an excellent method of selective viewing, however after several years we relented and moved it to the playroom.

The central attic room became a play area for snooker and table tennis. A tiny room at the top of the stairs provided our eldest daughter's bedroom, a bolt hole from her siblings. It is still used by her when she visits, an escape from her own children.

Although they have all fled the nest and have homes of their own, their rooms are still here for them and used when they stay, often accompanied by their families. These attic rooms have a parapet outside their dormer windows, much enjoyed by the children. One Christmas morning when in the kitchen I saw two bodies abseiling past the window! It did look great fun but so far I have not tried it, neither have the grandchildren but I expect it is only a matter of time.

With the reroofing of the house in 1969 John decided to raise the ceiling of these rooms thereby exposing the old oaken beams, a rewarding and dusty exercise, but making them more useable and habitable. They are still used occasionally as dormitories when the house fills up for Christmas and parties.

The refurbishment of the house gradually progressed and in 1965 when Hal, the last of the five children, was born, he had the luxury of a nursery to himself.

Garden creation and maintenance has always occupied a fair amount of our time, never having, as yet, employed a gardener. Whenever the weather was good and indoor demands not too great we would go outside and do battle with the weeds. When we arrived at Nazeing Bury the East garden had been used as a dumping ground for spent mushroom compost which promoted a profusion of docks and convolvulus. Phil McAleer was a superb dock digger and we had competitions to see who could produce the longest roots. Bindweed covered four erstwhile rose beds in the front garden. This we removed and reinstated the beds. There were the remains of a pond from which we removed the base to create another bed, ever since planted with iceberg roses; battling against the bindweed has remained a continual war of attrition. We then planted a yew hedge to the south of these beds.

Some time later, on the sound advice of my mother-in-law, we fenced off an area on the west side of the house and made a small private garden, which can now be approached from the study (my hoped for Edwardian drawing room) in which John made himself a small pond for the sound of plashing water. This is more manageable than a larger pond in the east garden I dug with the help of a friend, which was later extended and deepened by one of our sons. We now have "his" and "hers" ponds.

In the gale of 1987 a very large weeping willow was blown down and we lost many fences. In the next gale to hit southern England the rather ugly carport was literally blown away and mostly deposited in the back garden. This really was a favour as John's brother designed a new one, a greatly improved structure with a hipped and tiled roof.

In 1991 we built a conservatory on the north wall behind the dining room replacing an ugly glass lean to. This has been most successful as in this situation we do not fry in the summer but can enjoy the sun, especially when it is westering of a summer's eve. We are still making changes in the garden and hopefully enhancing it.

Originally there was a large greenhouse attached to the shed at the back of the house. Here for two years we grew green peppers and sold them to a greengrocer in Hoddesdon. Not a wildly successful financial endeavour but at least it was being used, until the glass succumbed to wind and flying objects. We then moved in an old chicken house that had belonged to John's mother during the war and I started keeping chickens and later ducks. This I loved and it was wonderful to have fresh eggs, but we did have problems with foxes so erected a high wire fence. We also kept rabbits and guinea pigs as childrens' pets. With this motley collection I also had a Canada goose called Karsh who, after four years, started laying eggs. There were two Aylesbury ducks called Donald and Daisy who wandered freely and sometimes had to be removed from the waiting room since not all patients were enamoured of them. On two separate occasions we brought lambs back from Wales and reared them mostly in front of the Esse. In spite of this luxurious start in life they were eventually integrated back into their Welsh flock.

Much of my own childhood was during the Second World War. My sister and I were evacuated for most of these years and therefore unable to have pets. My first pet was a cat given to me when I was thirteen, I loved her dearly and made a decision that if and when I had children I would let them have any pets they wanted - barring snakes. This the children took full advantage of over the years and we all thoroughly enjoyed them. I myself bred King Charles Cavaliers for twenty years, they are splendid and amenable little dogs to have with children. When they were having their puppies John took the opportunity to give biology lessons to the children and their friends. We have still two old Cavaliers and John has his beloved chocolate Labrador given him by the children on his retirement. Cats we always have, and kittens often, for whom we somehow manage to find good homes.

Family Parties The house has been wonderful for parties of all kinds, we always feel it comes to life when filled with family and friends. We wonder whether previous dwellers here also felt this, as the photograph of the Pegrums Golden Anniversary with their sixty relatives suggests. In 1978 we celebrated the Golden Wedding of John's parents. A mere thirty of our relatives sat down to dine, few by Pegrum standards, but at least all our guests stayed the night. This was an occasion when all the bedrooms were filled and many young lined up nose to tail in the attic. Not comfortable, but most accommodating. Commenting on this happy occasion Papa later wrote: "What popping of corks to start the tongues wagging, the food was delicious, as was the Tokay. Some organisation!"

The first real party, I suppose, was to celebrate the christening of the first four of our five children. Hal's arrival being five years later he had an exclusive christening all to himself, in Tunbridge Wells. He was born in the house as was Nigel before him and I wonder how many other births the house has seen in its long history.

We went on to have many childrens' parties and then much larger and I fear rather more noisy affairs for eighteenth and twenty first birthdays as they succeeded year by year. We had discos in the hall and bands in the garden with barbecues for large numbers of young people. For some years we had bonfire night parties on November 5; these were great fun as they involved both adults and children, so pleased all ages. For a thirtieth birthday party we had a dinghy in the hall as a centre piece, being a present for one of our sons.

The largest family party was the marriage of our two daughters. A double ceremony was held at All Saints Nazeing, followed by a reception in a marquee erected on the front lawn at Nazeing Bury. Prior to going to the church we had an amusing little drama caused by the smallest of the four bridesmaids, Alison, then aged three, Bobby Sutherland's eldest daughter and my goddaughter. The four bridesmaids assembled in the hall awaiting the descent of the two brides from upstairs. When they appeared she let out a yell, not recognising them with their veils over their faces. She thought she had seen a pair of ghosts!

We had the church decorated with cream and multicoloured flowers and carried the same theme through the marquee and the house. The lining of the marquee was yellow and white stripes, so despite a day of pouring rain, within all appeared sunny. Everything looked wonderful against this background, especially the two brides. Thankfully the sun shone as the couples were about to leave on their respective honeymoons and we were able to have a group photograph, in the sunshine, of nearly all our two hundred and fifty guests.

Another event which made for more family parties was started following the death of Kate Cook, John's great grandfather's parlour maid. She was a splendid character who lived in Bath. She sent us bath buns at Christmas, knitted socks for the boys and kept her finger on the pulse of the Gervis family. When she died at a great age she left all her worldly possessions to the great grandchildren of Dr. Gervis, who had died in Bath many years earlier. We cleared her flat and having brought everything back here invited all the members of the family for the weekend and very fairly divided up the spoils, even her hats of which she had many. We had a wonderful time and because of this and of fond memories of her decided to make it an annual event. This we have done and a 'Kate weekend' as it is called, has been held here or at other family members' homes over the following years. These events are attended by as many family members as possible, sometimes from as far afield as France, South America or New Zealand. For the dinner on Saturday night we all wear one of Kate's hats. I think anyone observing this scene would be worried about our sanity! We have sometimes involved the next generation by inviting them on the Sunday for a larger party in celebration of Kate.

Besides our many family parties we held retirement parties for Freddie Beilby and Leslie Roe in 1985 and 1990 respectively. To these came everyone associated with the practice and their partners, past and present, including Ann Cayford our one time practice manager whose brothers had once inhabited the house. John's own retirement party was held at the Limes Surgery in 1993. All very enjoyable evenings but sad that the old order changeth.

In 1996 we gave a surprise party for our eldest daughter's fortieth birthday, an extremely well kept secret, especially by her own children and one to which they had been privy since its inception.Sunshine greeted her arrival as did, to her amazement and delight, forty of her friends and relations. Champagne corks popped and much food was consumed sitting at tables in the garden with background music and jollity from adults, children and dogs.

Christmas time is when the house really comes into its own. John and I both feel it is our favourite time, the log fires aburning, the Christmas tree lights ashining and the decorations aglow to be enjoyed by children, grandchildren and adults alike.

The House and its Place in the Village

We know that in the middle ages the Bury would have been used as a communal building for various activities, including the holding of the courts and I wonder whether, with its associations with Waltham Abbey, it might have been used in other public ways?

Our first big communal party in the house, and more especially the garden, was for Queen Elizabeth's Silver Jubilee in 1977.

We formed a small committee from the residents of Nazeing Road to organise this. On the day we set up tables in an E shape decked out in red white and blue bunting. We prepared all sorts of food and drink enjoyed by adults and children alike. This was followed by various games and entertainments. The children then participated in parades around the village whilst the fathers slept on the lawn in glorious sunshine and the mothers cleared up.

A similar atmosphere was evoked when we celebrated, in 1995, with the help of the church, the commemoration of VE day with a tea party as a re-creation of a post war street party. We had tables all down the drive, again decorated in red white and blue bunting and one hundred people were served tea with a menu of war time food, but hopefully more appetising. This was followed by games and a raffle. Some of the older generation who remembered the war dressed appropriately and brought memorabilia of that far off event.

Every year in June we hold a mini market in the garden in aid of the Nazeing Association for the Elderly and the Handicapped. This raises money for the association and other charities by means of stalls, side shows and raffles with coffee and cakes being sold in the hall. This makes a good venue for our members and other villagers to congregate and converse, especially when the sun shines.

For the last four years in July we have held a ‘Pudding Evening.’ We entertain around sixty five people with wine and delicious puddings, many prepared by the guests; followed by coffee and the inevitable raffle. Tickets for this event contribute towards funds for the Flower Festival which is held at All Saints in alternate years. This is a good event, especially on balmy evenings when we can sit and eat outside.

I hope so long as we remain here we will continue to host such functions. We both feel a certain privilege, living here as we do, really enjoying these opportunities of sharing the house with others. What fun it would be to be able to look back on past events. How did the people look? How did the house look through the ages? Recently Peter Huggins, a local archaeologist, suggested we lift the flagstones in the hall to see if there were any evidence of a central hearth or other artefacts of the distant past but we have no immediate plans so to do!

In times past the house stood isolated in its own fields, a moat around it, surrounded by what trees and wild flowers? Now we are an island, surrounded by buildings and roads but are endeavouring to keep the house and garden as a useful and peaceful oasis.

There is no knight in shining armour - or if there is, he does not wish to be seen by us. I do not think Mrs. Ramsey comes searching for her feather bed in her erstwhile bedroom. Perhaps I could come back and see the future owners of our enormous front door key? I promise to be a very friendly and non intrusive ghost.

On reading this through I realise I have ignored the darker side of life and have made it sound as if it has been continuous happiness, sweetness and light. This is untrue and very unlikely for any household. We have had our times of sadness and troubles, but thankfully we have so far managed to surmount them. Whether the problem has been the house or its occupants, ultimately we have benefited from its peace and solidarity. Or so it feels.

Finishing this as I began, in the heart of the house, there is still soup bubbling on the stove, but now spring is coming and we are planning further refurbishments for this year. Without this care, especially on John's part, ongoing since 1960, I doubt if there would be a habitable house for me to haunt in the years to come.

IN CONCLUSION

John Gervis

There have been times, I will admit, during our sojourn at Nazeing Bury when the house has felt like a millstone around my neck. Endeavouring to undertake the innumerable maintenance tasks, and pay for them, whilst at the same time coping with the fairly demanding life of a general practitioner and a father could prove wearing. Installing the central heating was a case in point. I consequently became a bit of a bodger, as my rather meticulous children would testify. But at least the jobs got done with the double spin-off of economy and a feeling of achievement. It has taken a little while since retirement to remember that I now have time to do things properly!

Margaret has been my invaluable arbiter where matters of taste have been concerned and we obtain mutual enjoyment of this house that we love. Without her active encouragement and help neither life at Nazeing Bury nor this book would have been possible.

We did not realise when we recommenced this search for the history of Nazeing Bury how much material was waiting to be discovered - the finding of which has been most satisfying.

By happy coincidence, as this study was being completed, the BBC showed the TV series *Be Your Own House Detective* which seems to confirm a wider interest in this subject of old houses and their histories.[1]

[1] See also BBC publication: *Be Your Own House Detective*

LIST OF ILLUSTRATIONS AND MAPS

Front cover, watercolour by Alan Hart, 1989	
Photo: Dr John Gervis and Margaret, 1995	3
Plan of Nazeingbury, late 17th century	12
Nazeingbury around 1800	12
Ground Plan of Nazeingbury, January 1997	13
Cross Section of Nazeingbury	14
Wall plate across south projecting bay	14
Cutlands, St Leonards Road, Nazeing	15
English and Flemish brick bonds	16
Floor joists	16
Photo: The Last Court Leet, 1925	30
The Maud Parr Indenture, 1527	36
Photo: The extended Pegrum Family, 1897	52
Map commissioned by Sir Wm Wake, 1767	58
Map by Chapman & Andre dated 1774	60
Ordnance Survey Map dated 1898	62
Photo: The River Lea near Broxbourne Bridge	66
Photo: Oak Beams in the Attic	76
Photo: Celebrating VE-Day in May 1995	90
Photo: Family croquet at Nazeingbury	90
Photo: Nazeingbury during reconstruction, 1986	100
Photo: Lodge Farm, Nazeing Common	100
Photo: The Gervis Family at Nazeingbury, 1996	116
Photo: Margaret, 1985	122

LIST OF APPENDIX MATERIAL

Appendix i	Chronological Tree	140
Appendix ii	Nazeing Bury Owners/Tenants	144
Appendix iii	"Vicarage" and "Advowson"	146

Appendix 1

Family Trees

Henry VII 1500 Sir Thomas Parr = Matilda (Maud) Green

d 1517 d 1529

Henry VIII 1510 William = Ann Bourchier Katherine = 1543 Henry VIII

1509 1512-1548

1520

1530

1540 **Henry Denny = 1 Honora Gray**

Edward VI 1540-1573 2 Elizabeth Grey = Edward Greville

1546 1550

Maryl 1553

Elizabeth I 1560

1558 **Robert** Anne = George Goring

1570 d 1576

1580 George Goring = Mary Nevill

1583-1663

1590

James Hay = 1 Honora

James I 1600 1st Earl of Carlisle

1603 1580-1636 = 2 Lucy Percy

1610 George Goring = Mary Burlington Ann died young

1608-1657

1620

Charles I Charles= Diana= Elizabeth= Mary=

1625 1640 Alice George Porter William Brereton Dru Deane

Cromwell 1650

1649

Charles II 1660

1660 John 4 Bt Baldwin 5Bt = 1 Ann Robert = Elizabeth

1670 1665-1747 = 2 Mary

James II 1680

1685

Owners of Nazeing Bury in Bold

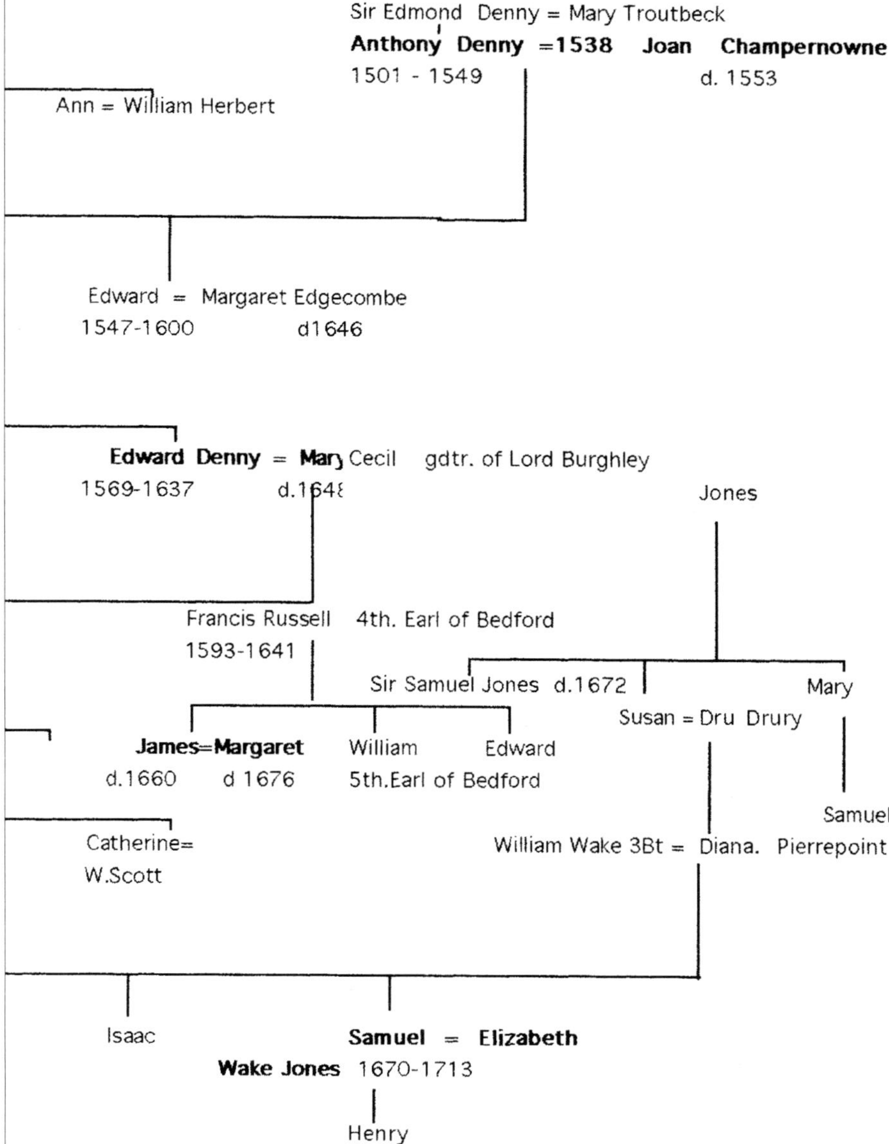

1660		Baldwin 5Bt = 1 Anne	Robert = Elizabeth	
	1670	1665-1747 2 Mary		
James II	1680			
1685				
William&	1690			
Mary 1688		Baldwin = Mary		
Anne	1700			
1702		**Charles Wake Jones**		
	1710	1701 - 1739		
George I			William Wake 7 Bt = Sarah	
1714	1720		1715 - 1765	
George II		**Charles Wake-Jones 6 Bt.**		
1727	1730	1725-1755		
	1740			
		William Wake 8Bt. =	Mary Fenton	
	1750	1742-1785		
GeorgeIII	1760			
1760		**William Wake 9Bt.** =	Mary Sitwell	
	1770	1768-1846		
		Old Sir William		
	1780	Built Courteenhall		
	1790	**Charles Wake 10Bt.** =	Charlotte Tait (brother: Archibald)	
		1791-1864		
	1800			
	1810			
George IV	1820			
1820		**William Wake 11Bt.** =	Margaret Fricker	
WilliamIV	1830	1823-1865		
1830				
Victoria	1840			
1837				
	1850	**Herewald Wake 12Bt.** =	Catharyn St Aubyn	
		1852-1916		
	1860			
	1870			
		Hereward Wake 13Bt. =	Margaret Benson	Joan Wake
	1880	1876-1963		1884-1974
	1890			
Edward V	1900			
1901		**Hereward Wake 14 Bt.** =	Julia Lees	
	1910	b1916		

1850 **Herewald Wake 12Bt.** = Catharyn St Aubyn

1852-1916

1860

1870

Hereward Wake 13Bt. = Margaret Benson. Joan Wake

1880 1876-1963 1884-1974

1890

Edward V 1900

VII 1901 **Hereward Wake 14 Bt.** = Julia Lees

1910 b1916

Appendix ii

Nazeing Bury

	Owner
1500	Monks of Waltham Abbey
1502	30 year lease to:
1540	The Dissolution. Thomas Cromwell
1541	Henry VIII. Leased to Anthony Denny
1547	Ralph Sadler. Alienated to Anthony Denny
1553	Leased, then gifted by Edward V1 to Joan Denny
1561	Henry Denny
1573	Robert Denny
1576	Edward Denny
1600	
1608	James and Honor Hay
1636	James, second Earl of Carlisle
1659	Edward Russell
1680	Samuel Wake Jones
1691	Samuel Wake Jones
1713	Charles Wake Jones
1739	Charles Wake Jones 6 Bt
1755	William Wake 8 Bt
1785	William Wake 9 Bt
1792	Leased to: Peter & John Leathers 1792
1795	Leased to: W,Welch 1795
1838	
1846	Charles Wake 10 Bt
1864	William Wake 11 Bt
1865	Herewald Wake 12 Bt
1881	
1916	Hereward Wake 13 Bt
1919	Purchased by Joseph Pegrum

Owners and Tenants

Date	Tenant	Source
1501	George Congreve	Wake
1502	John Nankotton, of London	Wake
1569	John Ramsey, d. 1569	Will
1594	Thomas Curtis, d. 1601	Par.Reg
1637	Payson, John	Par.Reg.
1660		
1672	William Foord	ERO
1709	Randolph Laurence	Wake
1740	John Lake	Court Rolls
	John and Ann Lake	Par.Reg.
1784	James Goodwin	Court Rolls
1798	James Goodwin	Court Rolls
1798	William Welch	ERO
1812	William Collins	Census & Wake
1838	Edward Collins	Census & Wake
1871	Edward Collins	Census
1881	Joseph Pegrum	Census
1919	Inhabited by Joseph Pegrum	

Appendix iii

The Vicarage and the Advowson

Readers may notice in the Wake documents recurring mention of the word 'vicarage,' often seemingly as an attachment to Nazeingbury. Spelled in several ways it crops up over a span of two hundred years. I have not quoted from them all. When I first read these I assumed the reference was to a physical building - the vicarage, as we currently use the word. But the meaning of the text becomes more explicable if the word is understood in its alternative financial sense rather than denoting bricks and mortar, namely: 'The benefice or living of a vicar.' Or to put it another way - the emolument due the vicar by means of the tithes levied. The tithes contribute to the upkeep of the vicarage, the levy for the church. Contained in the court rolls for the 18th century are the customs due the vicarage. These included: One tenth of all corn; 4 pence for a cow and calf; 3 pence for a milch cow and 2 pence for a fatting beast.

Antonia Fraser is most informative on this subject in her book on Cromwell, so much so that I quote her at length: "Long before the Civil War, for decades, centuries even, the issue of tithes had been controversial and there had been many disputes on the subject. Literally meaning a tenth or tithe of the produce and livestock of the parish, dedicated to the support of the local church, the tithe had come to symbolize a series of different - but equally emotive - things to different people... In many cases ***tithes had passed into the hands of temporal owners*** [my italics] at the time of the dissolution of the monasteries and the maintenance of the system had become part of powerful vested lay interests."

In the case of Waltham Abbey, after the dissolution the tithes passed to the crown and, after, to succeeding Lords of the Manor, commencing with Anthony Denny. Whether by the following century the vicar was actually receiving any of the tithes enumerated above remains uncertain.

Likewise the **rectory**, another recurring term, carries the double meaning of the 'freehold' of the living *and* the habitation of the rector, the appointee of the lord of the manor or the lord himself as lay rector.

In the 1541 copy of the lease to Sir Anthony Denny, inter alia he obtains the lease of the rectory of Nasynge and ***tithes***, my italics. When we come to 1641 the Earl of Cork is to have, 'the rectory of Nasing together with the viccaridge., in other words the tithes.

Sir William Wake in 1792 evidently leasesNazeingbury, together with the vicarage of Nazeing. It would seem therefore the landlords of Nazeing, in common with many in this era, were in fact pocketing at least some of the vicar's stipend. Its financial worth seems to be emphasised by the fact that it continues to feature in these indentures. The cash return in 1535 is given as around £14, £50 in 1650 and £70 by 1760.[1]

Cromwell, as Fraser comments, was well aware of the inequity of this system, but was not successful in his attempts to legislate on the issue. So now we turn to the Advowson.

The advowson is a term referring to the patronage of a benefice or living, the right to appoint and dismiss the incumbent. Until the dissolution of course this right rested in the Abbey but it then became appropriated to the crown, which in turn for most parishes passed on the right to the Lord High Chancellor. Even so inconsistency prevails. For example in 1622 we have the settlement by James, First Earl of Carlisle, granting during his life and then to his son:

> ...all that rectory of Nasing [Neither] rights nor
> advowson of the Vicarage of Nasing at Nasingberry.'

Strictly interpreted this would seem to mean no rights to either appointing the vicar or to his tithes. This seems slightly odd since the year before the Earl of Cork was granted by George Lord Goring, amongst other things, the viccaridge. Again in 1659 the younger James grants Edward Russell the rectory and the vicarage of the church of Nasing.

Even in 1792 William Wake was - in his own mind anyway - entitled to dispose of: 'the whole advowson of the vicarage of Nazeing.' i.e. to appoint the vicar. The Wakes as Lords of the Manor continued to occupy the position of lay rector, thereby entitling themselves to the benefice, the rectory, until this right was abolished in 1936.

[1] VCH vol v p 147

In [illegible] concerning the [illegible] being that kindly supplied by Brian [illegible] three occasions Nazeing Bury was [illegible]

Brian was a planning officer for Epping [illegible] has had a lifelong interest in the house [illegible] connection was [illegible] had [illegible] correspondence [illegible] He kindly [illegible] copies of all the documents [illegible] the house. Brian's father incidentally was at one time [illegible] of Nazeing Primary School.

I have mentioned in the book the [illegible] which [illegible] Reginald [illegible] himself [illegible] the land [illegible] Nazeing [illegible] had not [illegible] prepared [illegible]

In [illegible] informed [illegible] plan [illegible] R [illegible] for the erection of three [illegible] the house, Nazeing Bury. [illegible] building [illegible] which would have been [illegible] dwellings [illegible] [illegible] these plans [illegible] and purchased the house [illegible] demolition.

By these records [illegible] for the house [illegible] Company in [illegible] which was [illegible] by H M Vessels [illegible] some time [illegible] September 1941 [illegible] need of [illegible] that Nazeing [illegible] as well, provided they [illegible] [illegible]